Pathfinder

Selected Poems, Essays & Tales

Robert Love

Up On Big Rock Poetry Series
SHIPWRECKT BOOKS PUBLISHING COMPANY
Winona, Minnesota

Cover and interior design by Shipwreckt Books.
Wheel of Birds design for Confluence Timber Company
©Inez Love, 1995.
Cover background photo by

Shipwreckt Books Publishing Company
357 W. Wabasha Street
Winona, Minnesota 55987

Library of Congress Control Number: 2023930178

Contents

Pathfinder

THERE ARE PLANTS around here known as Pathfinders. They grow in the understory of open forests and in the fringes of wetlands, and have broad, flat, dullish-green leaves that turn and reveal their light green undersides when a bear, human, moose or coyote walks through them. So it's easy to see if someone's beaten you to the berry patch, paused to nip some alder buds or curled up to take a nap.

When I was searching for a title for this book, the spirit of this plant offered it to me. I accepted her gift with gratitude and wonder, instantly sensing its pertinence: the poems, essays and stories gathered here are upturned Pathfinder leaves, marking the literal and spiritual trail I've traveled, from the Appalachians to the Rockies, from the headwaters of the Ohio to our home on a tributary of the Columbia, from dour Scottish Presbyterianism to the sweat lodge and Sundance, from youth to old age.

At first I edited the pieces as I selected them. But then I realized that this was like backtracking, and re-arranging Pathfinder leaves; that extensive revisions would obscure the voice of the person who wrote them and blur the trail. So I decided to let him speak for himself, and hope he'll travel with me into the territory that lies ahead of us.

Introduction

In 1973, in his poem "Reply," Bob Love wrote,

All these years
I have been learning
the woods, and now
you call me a poet.

He's spent the 50 years since then working in the woods, and he's still learning them. He's a logger, and a conservationist. He speaks directly and with authority. The first 99 pages of the book are poems—presenting a crystal-clear tableau of a life well-lived. The rest of the book is a collection of essays and stories that fill in the gaps of what may have been implied in the poems.

I've known Bob since he started college in 1971. At a time when many budding poets were interested in modeling themselves after the Confessional Poets, Bob had a clear mature voice and wrote lean lines that looked toward poets such as Gary Snyder—not focused on the self but on apprehending the world outside the self—with clear eyes and an open heart. There was no point in trying out different personae, styles, and forms as he knew who he was and what he had to say—he was comfortable in his own skin. Many of the poems and essays in this book have to do with work—Wendell Berry, writing about working the land, was a poet for whom Bob developed high regard. He saw in Berry that one can be reverent without being sanctimonious. He and Berry have been corresponding for many years now.

In reading Bob's poems and in talking with him it was obvious to me that he listened carefully to master poets, took what he needed, and left the rest. He wasted nothing, just as he did when he hunted. In class discussions, he never said much but when he did express an opinion it usually cut through all the b.s. we'd been throwing around. I'm not sure that I taught him anything other than suggesting what he should read. And maybe the value of white space and the importance of what you don't say. He was always a quick study. At one point he was auditing my Modern Poetry class. I was lecturing on Ezra Pound and took some time with The Cantos, almost 900 pages with lots of obscure references and epigraphs in many languages. Bob came up to me after class a week later, and said, "I read around in that Pound book—it was pretty good stuff." He'd checked out the library copy of The Cantos and had digested samplings of it in a week's time—a prodigious task. There were several excellent students in that class, and although Bob wasn't even taking it for credit, he was the only one who had the curiosity and gumption to go below the surface of The Cantos.

As he states in his "Feral Shaman" essay, Bob's father and uncles were important mentors to him as hunters and fishermen. Though his father worked at a desk job, he was a dedicated naturalist and subscribed to several "hook-and-bullet mags" but also to several publications that were "more conservation-oriented and had a lasting influence on me." Bob had a sixth-grade teacher who showed his students the template left by the tribes that had inhabited that area of Pennsylvania. In high school, he took a course in Comparative Religions from a lapsed Jesuit priest that opened his mind to other ways of thinking and believing, especially Buddhism and the writings of Alan Watts and Lao Tzu. Many of his small poems, brilliant little gems, reflect both Lao Tzu and William Carlos Williams. Bob also garnered much from Scouting—in the classroom of the outdoors, that he still applies to his daily life and practices. He also pays homage to his grandparents in one of the essays. And there's a long essay about hunting with his son Orion. He honors the legacy of his forebears while presenting the gift of this book as part of his own legacy. It all started to fall into place, though, one day in church, when Bob was eight, during a Palm Sunday service; "The morning light was streaming through the stained-glass window ... and I could feel the breeze flowing ... I smelled greening grass and snow-rotted maple leaves. I heard a robin and a barking dog. There were some silver maples growing in the narrow yard between the church and the street, their bare branches silhouetted behind the stained glass. I was taking all this in when another question came to me: What was the religion of the people who lived here before us?"

There are some outstanding love poems to Bob's wife Inez, from the time of their courtship, such as "Explanation" (1974), to the day-to-day rhythms of work and family life, as in the poem "Wild Strawberries" (1993). The love poems express genuine reciprocal love and demonstrate what successful marriage and childrearing are all about. In relationships there must be dialogue, one must listen, whether it be between humans or between humans and non-humans. "Wild Strawberries," as with many other of these poems has the same clarity and groundedness as poems by Chinese poets of the Tang Dynasty. "Sweet Clover" and "Fall Equinox" are love poems that focus on the seeming routines of domestic life and strike deep chords. "Signature" is the most recent of these love poems and the most telling. In the hands of a lesser poet, these poems might turn sentimental or abstract.

I've known Inez for as long as I've known Bob; in fact, I stood up for them when they got married. Inez is a sparkling and talented person. In this book, Bob chronicles their living circumstances, from tipi to dirt-floor cabin to a full-fledged house sans running water or plumbing. In fact, in my office, I have a framed photo of Bob and Inez standing in front of their one-room dirt-floor cabin. It is winter. Inez is holding baby Orion. My younger son is also named Orion. And finally, an expanded house with plumbing and running water. I visited them in all these situations, and I have to say that they seemed content whatever their living circumstances. Their house, for which Bob sawmilled a good share of the lumber, is beautiful, and carefully designed in every respect. Bob also has his writing shack, a building that most people would be satisfied with as a primary dwelling. Their house has a spring-fed creek running along behind it, occasionally dammed by beavers, and they are a short distance from the North Fork of the Flathead River. On the other side of the river is Glacier National Park.

Bob is actively engaged in the Blackfeet culture. This association began 25 years ago when he was invited to a sweat lodge ceremony on Little Badger Creek. In 2013 he pledged to dance in the Yellow Kidney family's Sun Dance Lodge and continued doing that until 2018 when he retired from dancing. Since then, he has been learning other aspects of the Sun Dance ceremony so he can help the dancers fulfill their vows and help their families support them.

Some of his essays explore Forestry. He explains that he was a contract timber faller for skyline logging operations for 25 years until he could no longer tolerate in good conscience how he and his co-workers had been "harvesting" the forests. He says "Now, instead of making demands from the forest, I ask what it can provide. I'm focused on what's left instead of what's cut. I try to repair mistreated forests and help bring neglected forests back into balance, knowing that my understanding of their ecology is limited."

Bob is a believer in hunting magic and had been long before his connection with the Blackfeet; the poems are infused with examples of this. In his essay Fading Trails," he discusses a remarkable dream he had in which a cow elk appears before him in camp the night before a hunt and as he is about to shoot, she transforms into a human about the age of his daughter. She speaks to him and then an entire tribe of Elk People shows up and tells him that his role is to be the hunter in the communion between them. It is a very moving experience for him. This dream is reiterated in his essay "Communion" which was published in Bugle, the magazine put out by the Elk Foundation. In "Good Hunting," a letter by Dan Crockett, editor of Bugle, he says that some readers were so incensed by the essay that they canceled their subscriptions—they wanted nothing to do with that kind of "hoodoo-voodoo." Crockett closes his letter by quoting Jim Harrison: "Perhaps it takes a culture as slippery and venal as our own to discount the dream life that was so vital to people for 30,000 years."

Partway through Fading Trails, Bob says, "We should all be thankful that the spiritual affinity between animals and humans is being nurtured, like an ember in a dying fire, by a few people living in the remnants of hunting cultures that still exist." The last three stanzas of the poem "Big Hole Afternoon" show us the poet praying after a successful hunt. The first lines of these stanzas are as follows: I thank the Creator for this elk … I thank the Creator for this hunting ground ... And I thank the Creator for this good day/and friends like you/ to share it with." This is neither phony sanctimony nor cultural appropriation.

Dreams are another important aspect of Bob's life. Often animals will come to him in dreams and guide him through predicaments. He can always count on herons, ravens, and occasionally a coyote or an eagle to perform this function. Dreaming and reading the signs that occur in nature. Paying attention. Until you've been there this may sound like New Age hooey but think again. For a little context—the members of the Nez Perce nation acknowledged Chief Joseph as a chief, but specifically as a "dreamer," one who has the gift of seeing the future and crossing to and from the Other Side. And communicating with it. This was a distinct role within Nez Perce, and other indigenous cultures.

There's not much in this book that is derivative; however, the poem "Bailey Hill" compares favorably with William Stafford's most famous poem "Traveling Through the Dark." Both poems revolve around an animal that has been hit on the road and the poet is deciding what to do with it. Bob's poem has much more specificity.

The "Saskatchewan Waters" poems round out the poetry section and take us into a world a little wilder, as Bob and several canoeing companions make a canoe trip periodically into a remote area of northern Saskatchewan. The poems have even less fat on them than usual. One senses that this voyage is a welcome respite for these men.

There are three pieces that demonstrate Bob's relationship with his community, particularly with his extended family— "A Few Words for Our Friend Bud Moore," presenting Bob's eloquent words said at the funeral of Bud Moore, a logging, hunting, and lifestyle mentor, as well as soulmate and best friend. The poem "Blessing" recounts a blessing before a meal said by Bud Moore. And then there is "Ceremony" which tells in powerful detail of the sickness, passing, and funeral of Bob and Inez's friend Kerrie. The burial takes place in a natural setting of her own choosing. It describes the manner in which she dies, the details of how she is prepared for burial, and what is said over her as she is lowered into the grave. People would not be afraid of dying if they had friends like this.

Bob Love is an old soul. There is a reverent tone in many of these pieces, and mysteries abound. There is great power and intelligence in his words. But don't get me wrong— there is also a strain of wry humor that threads throughout the book. "Work Truck," "Reading Bukowski: Lunchbreak" and "Saw Shop Dharma" are three prime examples. And the poem "If" measures up to all the other poems that have been written extolling the lifestyle of bears vs. humans. To do justice to the myriad other salient aspects of the book would take an entire volume. Bob Love has kept relatively quiet these past 50 years and is now breaking bread with us, the larger community. You may have gathered that he is, by nature, a modest man, yet if we encourage him surely there will be a Volume II. Bob Love's audience will expand exponentially as soon as people get their hands on this vital book. There is much to learn from *Pathfinder*, but as Bob says in the short poem "Don't Follow Me"—

> *Don't follow me in the woods....*
> *Better to follow your own path.*
> *that way we'll cover more country*
> *and find more berries.*

—*Ken McCullough*
Winona, Minnesota
February 2023

Selected Poems 1973 - 2022

October Storm

Night sifts into this wind-bent house
 with the patience of sand.

On the lee side of a cottonwood
 there are withered leaves.
In the fields
 precise snowdrifts.

Red coals fall through the stove grate
 and fade to ash.

I have watched the seasons pass here.
A day is only the taut line
 of a falling star.

Turning back upon myself
 I will carve this knife with its own blade
and possess its magic.

Hyalite Shack 1973

Will's Creek

A wisp of dust
kicked from the bridge
feathers down and
whipsnaps
on a green muscle of water.
A feeding brook trout
darts from my shadow.

Glencoe, PA. 1973

The Storm's Gift

I
slit him open from tight gristly scrotum
 to ribcage
steam rising in a sheet
like snow blown from the needles of limber pine
thrust numb hands between his pulsing stomach
and firm liver
sudden heat pricks each cell with fire

looked up into the gray swirling sky
and said a prayer
kneeling in the snow
guts come free with a gurgle of dark blood
that streams over his flanks
thickens between my fingers
and tastes like sharp iron

intestines writhe like a beheaded snake
in the unexpected open air
color fades from his freezing eyes
that last saw me standing over him
terrifying instrument of final night in my hands

II
even after I had finished
the red muscles of his inner thighs
still twitched

Bridger Mountains
November 1973

13

East Of the Mountains

I
sage frost
half moon
blood dawn
ground sparkle
stomach numb
fingers burning
frozen to the earth
like a rock

antelope
my eyes
my eyes
are filled with light
flick your tail once
a mile away
they will find you

hear me
my ribs
are bruised
my elbows
my knees
cactus-torn
. you can't see me
slinking over the prairie
like a coyote
I am the sagebrush
I am a burned rock
I am the sand
that clouds behind you
that falls emptily
into your hoofprints

too far
far away
to see
but I know where you are
my Medicine
leads me to you

II
you feel my presence
graze nervously
on the knife-edge skyline
but you don't see me
flat in the rocks
on the lip of this coulee

I will lie here forever
to make myself invisible

I circle
crawling along dry creek beds
in the nightcool shadows
of windworn sandstone
not even a bird sees me
with the wind in my face
and the sun behind me
I stalk you
silent and inconspicuous
as death
so close I can
smell you feel you

breathing in the
tense morning

Brother
I am sorry that you die

III
this time
blood falls onto your trail
for the last time
the wind blurs your vision
and roars in your ears
for the last time
you lead your band
moving like water
to the end of the world
for the last time
your nostrils flare
your lungs explode
your tendons
become taut as bowstrings
answering the terror in your brain

but you falter
your legs quiver
you choke on your thick blood

the earth pulls you down slowly
whispering to you
die
fall here
return to me

Big Porcupine
October 1972

Reply

The poetry meeting was
drunk. The city lights
were like arrows, and I
couldn't see the stars,
so I came home.

Smoke rises from
the chimney like a
strand of hair,
splitting itself
to nothing.
I crawl into the
sweatlodge and sit
nameless in the separate
night. The rocks in the pit
are cold and the grass
breathes salt. I search for
a song, but all I hear
is my own voice.

All these years
I have been learning
the woods, and now
you call me
a poet.

Bozeman
November 1973

Explanation

The poem you wrote to me
has been folded with some papers in
a book, and I have to tell you
I haven't had the strength
to open it and read it again.
It is like the closet door of my
childhood that I would close each
night. The one time I read it my bones
felt like they were being split
by blue ice. I told you I was wild,
and had no money, that your absence was
like a hole in my side. You said you
wanted to be a bird that flew into me
from a high place, that you loved the
moonblood in my veins, that I should shed
my memory of you, like a snake leaves
his skin in the fork of a tree.
But my dreams bring you to me.
When I wake in the morning, your
warmth and scent are in the blankets with me,
and it's not until I've started the fires
that you vanish, like a star at dawn.

If I had the magic I would make you
my breath, and exhale you into a buckskin bag
that I would tie around my waist. Then I would
follow a stream to its source in the slabrock,
where I would open the bag and inhale you, and I
would breathe you out as a pool of water, into
a stream-worn bowl in the granite, in the shade of
a juniper. And I would become a coyote and
lap you up with my red tongue. With you inside me

we could travel safely. Even the ravens wouldn't
notice us. I would make rain fall behind us
to erase our trail, but there would always be sun ahead.
After a long journey we would come
to the right place-it would be as if
we had flown there. Then I would draw you
from my stomach into my veins, and slice the palms
of my hands with a crescent of obsidian,
and I would raise my arms to the sun and pray.
As the blood flowed, you would appear,
your hands flat against mine,
the sun warm between your shoulder blades.

And far away, where a buckskin bag
hung from a juniper limb, all of the past
would be standing, confused,
staring at the thunderheads in the distance,
lightning flicking from their bellies
like snake tongues.

1974

Slough Creek

We ride on the old trail
following each curve of the river,
crossing it where the trail crosses
over gravel flats scattered with driftwood,
and sandbars where hoofprints
collapse into themselves.

In the sage meadows
granite dust rises behind the horses,
just as it did when
the People rode this trail to the Obsidian Cliffs
to gather the rock that mirrored
the clear black gleam in their eyes.

But the Old Ways are gone,
like the scent of bruised sage
that grows faint on our backtrail:
Fires can no longer burn themselves out between rivers.
Game is scarce, and too wild for the bow.
Ancient migration trails are blocked.
The winter grounds aren't trampled and root-torn.
The ridge saddles show few tracks.
Spiderwebs are unbroken over the waterholes at dawn.

The Old Ways are gone, and people say
What good is it to remember?
They are like an eagle that has flown out of sight.
But somehow we still see him,
a fire with wings, eyes of blue sparks,
a constellation shining through a prism of flaked obsidian,
showing us the trail we should follow.

for Mr. Tamburelli (Tammy) 1975

Lodgepole

Lodgepole knots
burn blue.
Lodgepole smoke
swirls up through the
lashed poles,
weaving shadows on the canvas.
Lodgepole sparks
ride the current,
fading into starlight.

Obsidian flakes glint in the firepit;
the only trace of the Old Ones
who lived here. Their tipi rings
are grassed over. The travois trails
have been blurred by elk hooves.
But spirits share our fire,
and a prayer:
Lodgepole,
Thank you
For these flames
that warm us,
For the sweet smoke
that scents our hair,
For this limber ribcage
that shields us
from the sudden rain.

Cache Creek Camp
September 1975

Beginning

the rain washes everything clean

magpie and flicker
 cry at each other
killdeer and ground squirrel
 whistle back and forth
paired mallards wade in watercress
 and turn up their heads
when I walk past

spring rain meets itself on flat water
            mirrored

            cloud
              to
            cloud

May 1978

Wild Strawberries

We've had days of unsettled weather.
Even this late in June, there's a fire in the stove.
Our children are out picking wild strawberries,
And I'm trying to write a poem for a friend who has
    died.
The typewriter is dusted with lodgepole pollen
And words can't tell my dream.
I'd like to go into the mountains
And sit for a few days,
But tomorrow
I'll wake up hours before dawn,
Lace my boots,
And head for the woods again.

The children return,
Their fingers stained with strawberry juice,
The scent of larch smoke and rainy wind
In their hair, slamming the door,
Laughing, shedding clothes on the run,
Blessing our home with their racket.

Why does my mind go in circles
When it's all right here
In front of me?

6:28:93

Cinders

I
Grandpa died in midwinter. I hadn't yet turned two.
An ice storm hit the night before the funeral.

You woke early, left before dawn,
and spread cinders on every grade
between Rockwood
and the cemetery
at Glencoe.

When you returned
yellow furnace smoke
shrouded the waking town.
Caustic mist rose from the Casselman,
fouled with mine acid, the pools
where Grandpa and Uncle Winfield
once caught smallmouths
now the scarletorange of merthiolate,
the river a garish trail,
bleeding into the Youghiogheny and Monongahela.

After the funeral
we followed the hearse
down to the Water Level Road.

Our tire chains splintered the deckplanks
of Cox's Creek Bridge,
spiking the Ford's heater air
with the tang of frozen creosote.

At the summit near the Distillery
blue jays flashed in the laurel.
Greenbrier cloaked gray boulders.

In the bottoms near Cook's store
lean whitetails watched us
from the brambled edges of corn stubble.
Goldenrod stalks poked through the slats
of driftwarped snowfences
strung across sidehill pastures.

Up on the mountain
the red graveclay was frozen to flint.
A heartless wind mangled the preacher's sermon,
scattered his words like buckshot,
sheened red cheeks with frozen tears.
Winterleaved white oaks
in the picnic grove
buzzed like timber rattlers.

Coming down from the mountain
the ice melted to slush,
muting the ring of the tire chains.
You stopped on each hillcrest
waiting for everyone to make it.
Sitting in the Ford's back seat
swathed in the warmth
of damp wool
I drowsed to the hum of crossbars
grinding the coalcinders to ash.

When we got back to Grandma's
you carried me in from the car,
your suede jacket and buckskin gloves
steeped in Chesterfield smoke.
Her house was as empty
of my Grandpa
as I will always remember it.

You might say I was too young
to describe all these details,
that I just invented them from Grandma's
telling of how you spread the cinders.
But I had a dream, sixty years later,
that I want to share with you:
At the cemetery that day
I was standing in the shelter of Mom's winter coat.
I saw a man walking back and forth behind everyone,
peering over their shoulders.
It was Grandpa,
curious about what was happening.

II
When you died
the edge was off the summer's heat,
but the air was still hazed with chlorophyll.

I'd been so far,
so long, removed
that I couldn't get my bearings;
didn't know if the Pirates
were in the pennant race,
or what cutting of hay
was windrowed in the shorn fields.
Walking out behind the house
I noticed how the timber had grown taller,
and how the woods, once wilderness to me,
seemed smaller.
The old trails were brushed in,
but they found me
and led me along.
I knew all the plants
but couldn't name some of them.

I barely recognized you
in the cancered corpse at the funeral home.
But I saw your spirit:
luminous in the ceiling corner
above the casket;
you smiled at me like you did
when I had nightmares
and asked to crawl into bed
with you and Mom.

You didn't come to the church service.
I couldn't blame you:
the stained glass was gaudy
in the afternoon light,
the organ annoying, as usual,
the grief laden with too much perfume.

I sat in the front row,
near some wildflowers
that Amanda and Colby
had brought from Laurel Ridge,
and recalled a place where
those flowers bloomed this time of year—
there was the smell of dried ferns
rotting to soil under sandstone ledges,
water weeping from an anthracite seam,
warm rain greened by beeches,
yellowspotted newts
slithering on slick shale—
and I thought:
If only, just once more,
we could shiver against dawn
hunting fox squirrels,
or fish for brookies in the Blue Hole.
If only you could show me again

how to filet a walleye or gut a whitetail.
If only we could watch
the hardwoods turn their leaves
to a lowering sky
and I could hear you say, one more time,
"I love storms."

If only I could have
brought you flowers
or spread cinders on the road.

1989-2020

Blessing

Sunday afternoon, midwinter,
We join hands around the table.
Flames lap at the hearthstones
Like water curling over argillite.
Spliced in the corners, the cabin logs
Mirror our entwined fingers.
Purlins and rafters, grafted to the ridgepole
Rise and arch over us.

We bow our heads to Bud's prayer;
   Thank you for bringing us together again,
   Thank you for this food,
   May we use it to do good work,
   May we have kindness in our hearts.
The prayer flows through our hands
As our lives flow through the land.

Blinking through tears,
I look out the window.
Evening falls into the snow-shadowed forest
The sun slips over Hemlock Point.
Two whitetails cross the pond ice.
A red squirrel in a fir tree
Shucks one last cone before dark.

Blessed beyond belief,
Can we ever be grateful enough?

for Bud and Janet
January 1998

Inuya

    I walked into the storm
Bears let me pass
    I walked into the storm
Mule deer watched from their beds
    I walked into the storm
Glacier lilies glowed under the snow
    I walked into the storm
Gray wind roared in the Whitebarks
    but around me it was calm

    I walked into the storm

Inuya Pass
June 1998

Pacific Front

Nothing sharpens the scent
Of a cottonwood bud
Sliced by a ski edge

Like March sunlight
Cooled by a million
Melting snowflakes

That were flecks
Of seafoam
Four nights ago

Someone

hears robinsongs
muted by rain

    I'm

    still dreaming

3:28:00

Guess What Happened

When I left home this morning
A cold breeze drove the dry clouds east.
I didn't think I could get the last burning done,
But there was new snow at the jobsite
And a strand of smoke
Rose from yesterday's ashes.

I said a *thank you* for my good fortune
And got to work.
The coals held enough heat to kindle the slash
And before long I had fire.

While I was feeding it
A coyote appeared and said, "You're welcome."
Then he lifted his leg,
Peed on the beargrass,
And went on his way.

Snow steam rose with the sun
And I pictured each coyote track
Becoming a cloud.

When I walked in the door this evening
I wanted to say,
"Guess what happened today!"
But I didn't want to jinx this poem,
Which I'm giving to you
Because you know there's luck in coyotes.

Why else do the bats flit around you
When you play your cello
At dusk?

Why Picking Huckleberries is an Exercise in Mindfulness

Because
when your eyes
outrun your fingers
all you get
is leaves.

The First Poem

The first poem you write
at a birch desk
in a pine-paneled cabin
built for writing
should honor the trees you used
and the labor that yielded their lumber.

This poem
like the desk and the cabin
should be well-crafted
and practical.

It should consecrate
the work that will follow
but concede
that writing a poem
may be an excuse
to sit at a birch desk
in a pine-paneled cabin,
listening
to alder roots
sift the stream currents,
watching
Redstarts
feed in the willows.

June 2001

In the Ladies Section of JC Penney

after Pound: "In A Station of the Metro"

Women flitting
through the dress racks
on Sale Day:
Chickadees at the feeder,
Siskins in the Mountain Ash
dusting the snow with seed husks.

Big Hole Afternoon

for Gary and Mary

Camprobbers perch on axe-hewn vertebrae
And pick fat from the quarters
Hung on the meatpole.
Blood glazes on the packframes.
The low sun, blued by pinesmoke,
Draws the cramps from our legs.

I thank the Creator for this elk,
Sustenance for family and friends.
May her spirit shine in our eyes.

I thank the Creator for this hunting ground,
Its forests veined with bunchgrass and sage,
And the morning breeze, scented with whitebark and
   granite.

And I thank the Creator for this good day,
And friends like you
To share it with.

11:24:99

The Prize Winner

Last night we watched the
Pulitzer Prize-winning poet
read a poem on PBS.
He mouthed the words wistfully,
like he was eating hospital oatmeal,
and he grinned like a cut cat
when the interviewer swallowed it too.

He was a professor somewhere;
I pictured him walking across a campus
in the green light of maple shadows,
sitting in his office, writing a poem
about some other professor's poem.
I wondered if his wife ever pestered
him about tracking mud into the house
or leaving sawdust on his pillow.
or if he owned an axe.
And I thought:
what we need is poets with some bark on them,
half-deaf, arthritic, calloused and scarred.
Poets who don't chase prizes
or know where to find them,
but could use the money.
Poets who write poems that taste
like Glacier lily bulbs
seasoned with quartz flakes and spruce resin,
or elk backstraps
washed in snow, sliced thick and fried hot
on a tin stove glowing with pinefire
in the corner of a wall tent.

If poems tasted like that

poets would earn their keep.
They would be useful again.
They wouldn't have to convince us of their worth
by passing prizes around to each other.

April 2002

If

If I was a bear
I wouldn't have to carry an extra shirt
   or a fire-starting kit
      or a lunch
   In fall
      fat would ripple my fur
   In winter
      I'd sleep with my paws over my nose
   Skunk cabbage
      would be my first meal in spring
   And in summer
      an elk calf would tide me over
         until the Juneberries ripened
If I was a bear
I wouldn't have to make offerings
   to animals I killed
      or plants I used
I wouldn't question or judge anything
   I'd see things as they are
I'd be just as happy one place
   as another
If I was a bear
   I'd shinny up this buckskin snag
      crosshatched with claw scratches
   and make my mark
Just to say
   this is my home
      I like it here

Garry Ridge
1:26:03

Storage

This morning I built shelves in the shop,
Even though
I don't have much to put on them.

In the afternoon I sat at my desk,
Listening to a Redwing blackbird.

His voice was perfectly pitched
To the high water in the creek.
He told me
It was the first day of Spring.

I scrawled a few lines
On a scrap of paper
And threw it in the stove.
It seemed rude
Not to listen.

Some days
I just go through the motions;
Building shelves for things I don't want,
Crafting poems
Whose words won't hold my thoughts.

April 2004

Sweet Clover

At the place I'm working now
I built a landing in an old gravel pit.
There is sweet clover there
Growing beneath a cottonwood.
When I skid logs through there
It reminds me of
The summer we were married.
When I came down from the mountains
To see you at the ranch
On your birthday
I walked on the empty road
From Big Timber to Mcleod.
The scent of swathed sweet clover
In the hayfields
Gathered in the shade of the cottonwoods
Along the ditches
And the Absarokas
Gleamed as if
They'd been born that morning.

At that time
I never imagined
I could love you more.
Twenty-nine summers later
I see how naive that was.

6/28/04

Winter Range

After working all day
in the autumn rain
I loitered in the shower
hoping the heat would reach my bones.

I pictured the well pump
pulling the water through
glacial gravel, and driving it through the plumbing.
I thought of the turbines smoothly spinning
in Hungry Horse Dam,
drawing black water
from the flooded canyons
of Wounded Buck
and Lost Johnny.

I remembered a story my
friend Loren told me:
"The year the reservoir was filling
I followed some elk out of
Tin Soldier Creek.
They were headed across the valley
to their winter range on Horse Ridge.
When they came to the South Fork crossing
and found a lake, they pawed at the water,
milled around in the logging slash,
and turned back.
I followed them, but quit the track
when the snow got too deep.
I always wondered if they made it
through that winter, 'cause it was a tough one."

But nobody wants to hear that story
when they're loafing in the shower
after working all day
in the autumn rain.

October 2005

Between Dreams

For all we know,
stars are diamonds,
frozen in the bellies of glaciers,
etching trails across the bedrock of space.

For all we know,
there's another world beyond them,
where mountains like ours,
swathed in alder fields,
resist rivers of ice.

Walking Back to the Pickup

A few minutes ago
I saw an image of my
Cerebral aneurism.
I feel strangely privileged
To be diagnosed with such an exotic affliction,
But every day
Someone walks through this parking lot
With similar news,
Or worse.
Still, discarding
So many assumptions and expectations
So quickly
Leaves me lightfooted
And slightly winded;
Like when you finally
Make it back to the pickup,
Drop the tailgate,
And shrug out
From under a packframe
Lashed to a hindquarter
Of a raghorn bull.

8/30/06

Dumping The Ashpan

Blue, red and yellow,
Birch coals arc through
the night like meteors.

Hissing in the frost,
they cool to dust on Beargrass
and fallen Spirea leaves.

Veiled by thin cirrus
the Autumn stars
are as fragile as ashes
cooling to dust
in their own time.

October 2006

Mouse Trap

Barely visible on the crusted snow,
As if it had been etched by a feather,
A deer mouse trail, winding
From a slot in the woodpile
To a slab of fir bark
At the edge of the sauna porch,
Reminds me to turn the water buckets
Upside down on the bench
After I drain them, steaming,
Into the drift beneath the eaves.

Bailey Hill

On my way to work, a snowshoe hare darted from the brush
    on Bailey Hill.
I swerved to miss him, but he thumped under the right front
    tire anyways.
I pulled over and walked back to where he writhed on the
    road.
As I lifted him by the hind foot, his claws scratched the palm
    of my hand.
I carried him into the woods for the ravens.
The dank odor of his mashed paunch
and the frantic pulse of his tendons took me back fifty years,
to a sheared corn field in western Pennsylvania,
a Saturday morning in mid-October.
Frost steams to mist, fragrant with burnt gunpowder.
My father knocks the head of a kicking cottontail
against the barrel of his Ithaca to finish it off,
slits its belly open with his Case jackknife,
draws the guts out and wipes the blade clean on his pant cuff.
Holding the rabbit by the hind leg, I watch its intestines
squirm and gurgle on the tilled clay.
Its feet are grass-stained, and smell like alfalfa.
I hand the rabbit to Dad. He smooths its ears back like he's
    petting it, slides it into the game bag of his canvas coat, and
    we move on,
my brother and I birddogging through the blackberry thickets,
pushing the rabbits out to the stubble, into the guns.

I worried that killing the hare might be a jinx.
When I got to the job, I double-checked the oil levels on both
    machines
and gave them a thorough greasing.
I figured at the very least I would throw a track

or blunder into a hornet nest,
but there weren't any hangups, mishaps or breakdowns.
I made two phone calls from the woods.
One person said,
"How did you know I was thinking about you?"
the other,
"I was just going to call you."
It was one of those days when everything just fell into place.

Heading for home that afternoon
I drove down Bailey Hill.
A tuft of fur stuck in a swatch of dull blood
marked the spot where I'd hit the hare.
The aspens were empty of ravens.

8:31:09

Work Truck

When it was time to sell the Dodge
I considered washing it
but a cold front was blowing in
and I didn't want to risk freezing the hydrant.

I thought about straightening
the right rear corner of the bed,
bent when I backed into a dozer track
or a log deck, I forget which,
but decided that tackling the job
with my customary body repair tools—
a hi-lift jack, a comealong
and an assortment
of sledgehammers, prybars and wood blocks—
would just make it worse.

So I jammed the tailight into its mangled socket,
cinched it down with a couple self-tapping screws,
and wiped off the winter's roadfilm
with a musty sweatshirt I discovered behind the seat.

It's a work truck for Chrissakes, I muttered,
as I parked it by the mailbox and
duct-taped a chartreuse,
hand-scrawled, For Sale sign
in the driver's window.
Why try to doctor it up?

Walking back to the shop, I hoped
If I ever fell prey to an undertaker
He'd do the same for me:

Dress me in my woods clothes,
with my hands in the open,
exposing every stitch, scar and raw hangnail.
And don't bother straightening
the warped, aching finger
I always threatened to amputate,
but never did.

Commute

The radio yammers over the defroster.
No matter what,
The news is about money.
We worship Dow Jones,
Kill ourselves getting comfortable,
And waste time making comparisons.

The frozen alders
Along the road swath
Don't gripe about the weather:
They know longer days will come.

The elk on Teakettle Mountain
Browse on Pachistima
As the morning traffic buzzes in the valley.
Our racket doesn't disturb them.
Like us, they are born with it
And will die with it.

Ravens rise from a roadkill
As I pass the whitetail crossing.
In the mirror I watch them
Settle back to the carcass.
For them,
A pickup is as good as a wolf.

There's no mention of these things
On the morning news,
After the commodity reports,
Or on the talk shows
Where people berate their neighbors.

But as I drive I see how the land
Is like a wise parent.
It tolerates our rudeness,
Watching us pass,
One car after another,
One generation after another.
It lets us follow our own path.

April Storm

While the oatmeal simmers
I listen to the weather report from Calgary;
sub-zero in Peace River, ground blizzards near Red
    Deer,
black ice on Crowsnest Pass.

Here on the Flathead
the snow is more cloud than frost,
misting on the thawed grass.
Juncos search for grit in the woodshed
scratching through pinechips.
Chickadees flit around the empty feeder
demanding breakfast.

Out on the road
neighbors drive to work.
Slush slurs the clatter of Sam's diesel.
Swirling snow blurs the strobe
of the school bus.

I should get busy too.
There's brush to burn and
machines that need wrenching.
A shopful of shelved projects.
A bill from the bank
on the kitchen table.

But today I'll consider the wisdom
of the cottonwoods by the well
who are waiting for a better day
to open their tarred buds.

Let the world go about its business.
I'll take what the storm offers:
A morning to enjoy a cedar fire
while the snow slips off the roof.
A moment to rest
before beginning the task of summer.

April 2007

The Marten on the Gutpile

The ravens warn him
and scatter into the timber,
but the marten stands his ground,
perched on the cow's stomach;
his whiskers glossed with tallow.
His orange throat
smudged with blood

He retreats to a spruce limb
when we start skinning,
snarls at the camprobbers
who appear
in the absence of ravens.

They eat flakes of ribfat
while we bone the carcass
on the peeled hide.

I toss a slice of liver
to the marten.
He caches it under
a lodgepole windfall
and climbs back to his post,
growling deep
in his scrawny chest.

When we're finished
he watches us
squirm into our packs
and line out for the trail.

Before we're out of sight
he's nosing through the intestines,
haloed by jays.

Wise River
November 2007

Reading Bukowski: Lunchbreak

This is the most scuffed, torn,
dogeared poetry book
I've ever checked out of a library,
so I don't worry about taking it to work,
buried in the midden of spare wool shirts
and diesel-soaked gloves heaped
on the floorboards of the passenger's side.

Honoring tradition, I leave tracks for the next reader:
a smear of blood from a skinned knuckle,
a flake of huckleberry pie crust flecked purple,
ribbons of birchbark marking my favorites.

I wash the poems down with black tea,
straight, and chew on them
all afternoon.

Morning Chores

A blue heron
stalks brook trout
in the flooded canary grass.

I watch him hunt
while I brush my teeth.

His eyes are the green of wolf lichen.
His legs the yellow of willow bark.

His feathers absorb
the color of any sky.

This morning he is slate grey.

Sparse snowflakes
winnowed by alders
glaze his reflection
on the flat water.

Fall Equinox

A bull elk bugled us awake.

Inez said
"That's reassuring"
And got up to make coffee.

I hunkered into the blankets,
thinking
"That was the perfect thing to say."

He bugled again
as I shrugged into my shirt.

It was chilly enough
to merit a fire:
Birchbark and cedar
from the kindling bucket.
Lodgepole
from the woodbox,
pitch cured to amber
by the August heat.

A summer's worth of dust
scorched on the stove
while I mixed pancake batter.

I threw in a handful of huckleberries
we'd picked on Moose Peak.

They hissed on the griddle
steaming the windows
with storm clouds.
9/10/09

Four Elk Dreams

I

We were in our hunting camp.
Pine sparks flared from the stovepipe.
A cold breeze made my eyes water,
blurring the stars.
Elk milled around in the timber,
speaking with human voices.
The calves were playing and laughing.
Their mothers warned them,
"Hurry, let's go before the sun rises!"

II

I was trailing some elk in the snow.
Their tracks led to a cabin in the woods.
Hoofprints climbed the stairs and crossed a porch,
leading to a door of roughhewn fir.
When I knocked a man opened the door
and invited me in.
His wife and children, a girl and a boy,
were sitting at a table,
preparing to eat supper.
I said, "I'm following some elk."
He replied "Yes that's us. Please stay and share our
    food."
I sat down and ate with them.

III

I was hunting in high sage country,
following the rim of a sharp coulee.
A cow elk walked up from there.
She turned to face me.
I shouldered my rifle
and centered the crosshairs between her eyes.
I flicked the safety off
and slid my finger onto the trigger.
She turned into a young woman,
about the age of my daughter.
Terrified, I dropped the rifle,
apologized, and sobbed uncontrollably.
She smiled, and said
"This is how it is."
Then her relatives appeared,
and encircled me.
They started singing.
While they sang they were changing
back and forth, from elk to humans,
humans to elk,
in rhythm with the song.
They adopted me.

IV

I was hunting elk in the mountains.
I climbed until I came into some
bunchgrass parks edged with gnarly Doug firs.
Off to my right I saw the rack of a big bull.
He was lying there dead.
There was a bear on top of him,
guarding the carcass.
He was a Dream Bear,
larger than life, snapping his teeth

and slashing his claws at me.
Then to my left I saw another bear,
also on a dead elk, snarling at me.
Coming to my senses, I thought:
"I know better than this. I shouldn't
be hunting elk in the first place. How could
I have let this happen?"
The bears were warning me:
"Don't hunt elk! Don't even dream about it!"

2009-2020

Dream Poem

beneath ice
water

beyond sky
stars

within wind
air

other worlds
in this one

a dream poem
takes you
there

Hunting for Poems

When I was younger I hunted hard:
days on end, chasing old bucks,
passing up spikes and forkhorns.

Looking back, I see I was more concerned with
feeding my ego than providing for my family.

Now I'm grateful for any deer who offer themselves;
I accept the gift of their lives and thank them in my own way.

I don't chase poems anymore either.
I just watch for them.
If one appears
I don't ask too much of it.
I'm careful not to look it in the eye.

A few good words,
if they're the right ones,
are enough.

I've finally learned
that a yearling doe is better eating
than a Roman-nosed buck.

Raven Raid

Eleven moss-green
mallard eggs
harshly trephined;
yolk-smeared
shell shards
scattered
in the beargrass.

Breakfast dishes
on the table,
yellow splotches
in my blue bowl.

for Heidi, aka "Smartie Brown"
May 2011

El Niño

Their dam's submerged
but our beavers don't fret
they just leave higher stumps.

Dry grass is scarce.
The bluebird woman
weaves her nest with
moth wings and willow down.

Recreationists gripe about late snow
plugging the trails til August.
I think the mountains
could use some rest.

Rainbent maple shoots
arc across the cabin path
soaking my shirtsleeves.
Anyone else
would prune them.

June 2012

More Than a Friend

Opening a book
you loaned me
to find
flicker feathers
marking certain passages

(the same ones I would have
marked, only with
strips of birchbark)

I know
this journey
isn't our
first,
together.

for KC
Winter 2012

Morning Prayer

pine sparks echo
in the stovepipe

the ravens appear
for breakfast

if this breath
is my last

what's it matter?

birch buds
frozen now
will open
to redwing songs

1:25:14

Vacation

any time
I leave for a few days

I wonder if
the ravens,
not being fed,
will quit me

but when I return,
they appear,
waiting for me
to put some bread
on the scaffold

I need them
more than
they need me

but now, after
so many years,
I think they're coming
for something
besides food

Edit

I've spent half the morning
revising a poem written forty years ago.
The person who wrote it was a wild character.
He avoided switchbacks, trails and bridges;
just bushwacked cross country,
wading streams, threading
his way through brush and windfalls.
For him, the poem was good enough;
a trailsign that only he could see, marking
a place only he cared about. I'm backtracking him there,
watchful for the faintest trace: maybe a healed scar on an
    aspen, or a peeled
ribbon of larch cambium curled in kinnikinnick, or a fir
    sapling
with the limbs sheared off one side—signs you might think
had been made by teeth, claws or antlers—hoping to find
    something he
overlooked, left behind, or didn't know how to say at the time.

2:26:14

Contrary

You'd think the best way
to lure the Clown Spirit
into your dreams
is to sprinkle needles
from a lightning-struck piss fir
onto a stove lid ticking with pineheat,
and sleep with
a polka dot print
under your pillow.
But they don't call them
Contraries for nothing:
if you want crossed-up dreams
turn your back on that Clown Spirit,
tell him to go away and bug someone else.

That's when you'll wake up
knowing that part of your spirit is wandering.
You call it back with your morning smudge,
but it takes some time
to get your feet back under you.
And you wonder just what it is
you want from him.

July 2015

Feeding the Ravens a Road-Killed Snowshoe

downy hairs
lighter than snowflakes
lift in the wake of a wing

January 2016

MESSAGE FROM THE CLOWN
SPIRIT

BE YOURSELF
ACT FROM YOUR HEART
AND YOU'LL BE PROTECTED

PEOPLE WON'T UNDERSTAND
BUT THEN THEY WILL
SO DON'T WORRY ABOUT IT
BUT DON'T BE MEAN
BE TOLERANT AND KIND

YOUR SOUL IS ANCIENT
YOU KNOW WHAT TO DO

IT'S IN YOU
EVERYTHING YOU NEED
IS THERE
IN YOU

DON'T COMPLICATE THINGS
BY ASKING FOR HELP

Fasting at Two Medicine, May 2016

Welcome

the pike
who was hunting minnows
this afternoon
stirs in my belly
at the sound of surf
on the ledgerock

Churchill River
August 2017

Rain Dripping

Rain dripping
  from the eaves
Brings to mind
  a ticking clock
How to unlearn
  that association?

12/10/19

Not Dried Up Yet

Black smear of Molybdenum
on the windshield of the Timber Jack
brings to mind
the one-stroke calligraphy of a Zen Master
capturing the moment
when a raven flares her neck feathers

It's about time
I'm seeing things this way again.

9/30/2021
Tamarack Creek

Sky Burial

The chickadee
wipes the fat
from her beak
on the meat pole,
each side twice,
like she's honing a knife.

The spike buck
catches my eye
through hers,
the same way
someone looks at you
when they say goodbye,
before they turn
to open the door.

October 2004–July 2022

Don't Follow

Don't follow me in the woods:
if I step on a yellowjacket nest
they'll sting you.

Better to follow your own path:
that way we'll cover more country
and find more berries.

December 2022

Cheaters

I remember scoffing at the old guys
Who needed cheaters to file their chains.
When we teased them they'd
glare at us through scuffed, milky lenses
and say "Just wait. Your turn will come".

They were right.
It's my turn now.
It seems like I spend more time
hunting for glasses,
clawing through shirt pockets and glove boxes,
than it takes me to file a chain.
If I can't find them
"I just rub on it till it feels good",
like old Art told me forty years ago.
He must've been about as old then as I am now,
but still, when I file a chain
I sometimes wonder:
"Whose scarred, knob-knuckled hands
are these anyways?"

January 2023

File Handle

I could buy a plastic saw-file handle,
but I'd rather make one with a
deadfallen lodgepole branch
cut to length, drilled for the tang
and chamfered to fit my palm.

This morning when I pawed
through the clatter of bar wrenches,
rim sprockets, spark plugs
and raker gauges in the toolbox
a file handle emerged,
its pine-beetle scrimshaws
stained and highlighted
by bar oil, glove grease and sweat.

If I left it lying on a stump
a red squirrel might gnaw at the salt in it,
adding his artistry to the beetles'.
Or a deer hunter might toss it into his lunchfire
and warm his fingers with its flames.
If it endured several seasons of snow and sun
baldface hornets might build a paper nest
with the weathered sapwood.

A plastic file handle might work
as well as a lodgepole branch,
but if you lose one
nobody else can use it.

January 2023

Signature

This morning I noticed
one of our old textbooks on the shelf.
Skimming through it
I found a few poems that had left their mark,
but most of them were
convoluted, contrived, forgettable.
I wondered how I'd ever had the patience to read them,
bushwhacking through wordthickets
to find their meaning.
Now I can tell at a glance if
a poem's worth my time;
the same way I know
if a deer track's worth following or not.
So I don't read poems
that make me squint, or follow tracks that
won't put meat on the table,

When I tossed the book
into the give-away stack
the front cover fell open
and I remembered why I'd hung on to it:
there was your signature:
Shelley Markus,
a piece of art in its own right,
like a Clovis point sculpted from agate,
or the paintings of Lascaux,
timelessly elegant,
impossible to improve upon.
My body tingles when I look at it
just like it did the first time I saw you.
You captured me without trying,
or wanting to.

This poem can't possibly express the magic
I see in those thirteen letters,
but I'll staple it on the inside cover
of Naked Poetry anyways,
as my way of saying
that your signature is my favorite poem ever.

Winter Solstice 2022
for Shelley Inez, my Fire Sister

Saskatchewan Waters: Poems from Undercurrents: Impressions of a Northern Journey

Upriver

paddleflashes
mark the track
of a canoe
headed upriver
at sunset
along
the timbered shore

Catnap

According to our mythology
the seawater in my blood
tempered this bedrock
at its birth,
three billion years ago.

No wonder, then,
that its native warmth
makes me dream.

Rainbow Rapids

High Water

Running downstream on high water
you don't have to muscle the paddle;
just knife it in the current to stay straight.

When a whirlpool roils to the surface
your body flexes and veers with the boat.

Watching the shore go by:
red granite, white birch bark,
the bronze-green thickets of trapper's tea,
your mind drifts.

Where the river widens into a lake
you start working again,
and step back into the world;
searching for the next portage
or a good campsite,
thinking about supper.

Look at that raven playing with the wind:
his mind isn't penned in
by deadlines and maps,
his body's not burdened with tools.
Setting his wings,
he swoops and gives us the eye.
Flapping them twice,
he climbs, clears the timber
perches in a jackpine snag,
talks to us as we float past.

For him, the sky is water.
Clouds mark the currents
of the rivers he runs.
Cirrus River

Our Major Food Groups

Gruel and Jerky
for breakfast and lunch.
For supper,
Cornbread, baked in a pot,
and Whiskey, lightly watered,
used to cleanse the palate
of broccoli pasta in cheese sauce,
or other similarly insipid
storebought foods, before eating the main course of
    Pike,
caught and cleaned while camp was made,
and wolfed down
as quick as it's forked from the grease.

Turned Leaves Camp

Breakfast

The sharp
Wild taste
Of one
Black spruce needle,
Fallen into
The morning gruel,
Flavors the whole day.

That's why we're here!

Watching Stones Camp

Lunch

Venison jerky,
chewed with
fresh-picked
cranberries, blueberries
and an errant blackfly,
garnished with
a wisp
of caribou moss.

Instant pemmican!

Washed down
with teabrown
creek water.

Crosspole Portage

Supper

The pike's gills rise
when I make the first cut.
She twitches each time
the knife, sliding along her spine,
ticks a vertebra.
But her eyes look from a place
steel can't touch.
She doesn't expect remorse
or compassion.
This afternoon she was swimming.
This evening her flesh will fuel mine.
There's no need for apologies.
She never assumed
she would live in the same body
forever.

Cranberry Esker Camp

Someone Watches

Keep your voice down.
Don't point at things
Or hack the trees.

Hug the shoreline.
Even there
The water
Is blacker than obsidian,
Deeper than you
Might think.

Those boulders
Arranged on the ledge
Didn't get there
Accidentally.

Someone watches.

Ancestor Lake

Ceremony

Who knows
why there are so many loons
gathered in mid-lake.
At least twenty of them
yakking as we paddle by.

You'd have to
live here several lifetimes,
eat nothing but fish,
and never touch the shore,
to understand their language.

Ancestor Lake

Paddling In the Bow

You don't have to worry about details.
Watching the water curl around the blade
your thoughts wander, making poems.
With any luck you remember one
until you can write it.
It doesn't hurt to let the others go:
they cleanse your mind,
like water passing over a paddle,
making it new with each stroke.

Red Belt Lake

Broken Water

Rainbeads shine like stars
on the black lake.
In the space of one paddlestroke
the wind they carry
from the grey sky
foams on the whitecaps.

Dragonfly Lake

For My Paddle, A Gift from My Father Forty Years Ago

Funny,
Where
A riven
Sculpted
Ash plank
Can take you.

Standing Rock Lake

Last Portage

Last portage behind us.
We load the packs
And push off into the shallows.
No need for conversation.

After nine days out,
Our paddles slip through
The water like fishtails:
No splash or gurgle.

Listening to the bow wake
I hear
A strand of pickerel weed
Clinging to the keel.

Will the world
Be there
When we get to the car?

Turtle Lake

Essays and Tales

Signatures on the Land

"I have read many definitions of what is a conservationist, and written not a few myself, but I suspect that the best one is written not with a pen, but with an axe. It is a matter of what a man thinks about while chopping, or while deciding what to chop. A conservationist is one who is humbly aware that with each stroke he is writing his signature on the face of the land."
— Aldo Leopold, *A Sand County Almanac*

DURING TWENTY-FIVE YEARS as a logger and hunter in northwest Montana, I've made a few marks on the face of the land. I'm proud of some of them, and uneasy about others. While the logger's signature is usually more visible than the hunter's, they are both distinguished more by what is left on the land than what is taken from it. The trees or animals that are removed will eventually fold into other lives and forms, but the forests or herds that engendered them will be altered by their absence. This change may be either beneficial or detrimental, depending on what we take, or leave.

A couple of years ago I was selectively logging some property near West Glacier, Montana. The forest was predominantly Lodgepole pine. But numerous stumps in the area indicated that, prior to the Half Moon fire of 1929, it had been a larch forest, cut for railroad ties around the turn of the century. The loggers had left one larch because it was rotten. Fire-scarred, wind-racked and hollow, the ancient tree towered above the surrounding forest, even though it was barely half of its original height. Ravens used it as a lookout, and redtail hawks perched in it, watching for snowshoe hares. It provided sanctuary and food for insects, woodpeckers and cavity-nesting birds. Subsequent logging operations had removed the eighty-year-old lodgepole that had grown around it since the fire, and now a new generation of lodgepole encroached on the matriarch. In the process of thinning this doghair thicket I came across an occasional young larch and found more of them as I progressed. When I'd finished, these vibrant trees were exulting in the sunshine, and their parent seemed to be smiling down on us all.

The old larch was spared because it wasn't fit for lumber, but now it was one of the most valuable trees in the area.

The landowners told me that an elk herd used to winter here, but hadn't returned after poachers killed several of them. Maybe they'd shot the lead cow, erasing a vital piece of genetic memory, or maybe the survivors of the attack were traumatized, and decided to winter elsewhere. Whatever the reason, the land seemed incomplete without the elk. The signs of their life here were fading, yet poignant: powdery gray pellets scattered on the bedgrounds, black tooth-scars on the aspens, tufts of neck hair clinging to the pitch of an antler-rubbed lodgepole.

These traces evoked the same feelings in me as the larch stumps, and it occurred to me that the cutting of the larch and the absence of the elk herd are local versions of a story that is part of our national heritage. This history is documented in photographs of skinned bison carcasses littering the prairie, hunters and anglers posed beside sagging meatpoles, and forests stacked on railcars or jackstrawed in rivers. It's recorded in the journals of explorers, trappers and pioneers, and is brought up to date by the reminiscences of our elders. I've listened to the old-timers tell their stories and noticed that the land they describe bears only a superficial resemblance to the land I know. It's unsettling to think that many people accept this as a natural course of events and refer to it as progress.

Our treatment of forests and wildlife manifests a cultural assumption that inexhaustible resources will fuel infinite economic expansion. Consequently, our demands have exceeded the productive capacity of the land. In the process, rather than keeping people working on and connected to the land, we have adopted increasingly sophisticated technology and equipment which results in fewer and fewer people actually working in the woods. We need to think of land in Leopold's terms: as an organism, composed of collectively functioning soil, water, plants and animals. And we need to act accordingly. We have proven that we can log and hunt efficiently; now we have to learn how to do these things thoughtfully.

If we hope to leave whole, healthy land to our descendants, we have to foster and follow a philosophy of nurturing rather than exploitation, and communion rather than conquest.

I've tried to express this philosophy in my work, using parallels I see between logging and hunting. I've been fortunate to work with private forest owners who are receptive to this approach and have entrusted me with the care of their land. Thanks to them I've been able to translate my ideas into action.

I call it "Wild Forestry" because I honor and adhere to the natural processes that give the land its wild, original spirit. Deferring to nature in this way makes me more cautious and more appreciative of the complexity of interwoven connections that sustain us. Searching for these connections and trying to comprehend them is enjoyable and educational. When I observe the species, sizes and ages of a forest's trees, I can read its history and envision its future. When I study the shrubs, forbs, soil and wildlife, I get a more detailed picture. This is like following an elk trail. The information I read in the tracks is enriched by other signs: a chattering squirrel, a fir limb swept free of snow by an antler, a nipped maple bud. The more I see, the more I learn to see.

There are parallels between forests and elk herds that illustrate some basic natural laws. Healthy forests and elk herds are diverse, composed of a variety of age classes. The size of an elk herd is limited by the carrying capacity of its range, just as the number of plants in a forest is determined by climate and soil quality. In both forests and elk herds, predation and disease remove the infirm or unlucky. These individuals are like the interest of a trust fund and will be produced perpetually as long as the principal, or breeding stock, is preserved. The dominant trees and elk are reservoirs of proven genetics. Predators are the guardians of this reservoir; without them, fitness and health decline. In the forests of the northern Rockies, fire, fungi and insects are analogous to the lions, bears, wolves and coyotes that prey on elk herds.

Fire was traditionally the most powerful forest predator in this region. Like other predators, it formed interdependent relationships with its prey, co-evolving with topography, climate, plants, soils, animals and forest types. Native Americans burned to improve hunting conditions and wildlife habitat. Considering the degree to which our landscape has been altered by a century of fire exclusion, it is apparent that the Native use of fire was widespread and significant. In low-elevation, dry forests, fire frequencies ranged from ten to thirty years. These low-intensity cleansing fires burned the grass, brush and suppressed trees beneath the larger, more fire-resistant trees. This enhanced the growth of the dominant trees by eliminating their competition and protected them from catastrophic crown fires. Higher-elevation fires in moister forests occurred in one-to four-century intervals and tended to burn the entire forest. Mixed-severity fires burned mid-slope areas in a random, patchwork fashion that created forest diversity. In all cases, the chemical interactions of fires and soils rejuvenated grasses, shrubs and forbs.

Insects and disease become more prominent in the absence of fire, just as mountain lion and coyote numbers may rise when wolf populations decline. The aggressiveness of insects and disease is proportional to forest density. As density increases, sunlight and nutrients are more widely shared, increasing stress. Similarly, when elk numbers exceed food supply the health of the herd declines.

Our ability and obligation to temper our instincts with thoughtfulness distinguishes us from other predators. In the past two centuries, humans have become the prominent predator in North America. Unfortunately, we haven't acted with restraint or humility. The annihilation of wildlife and forests that characterized the 19th century was arrogant and malicious, while the zealous predator and fire suppression campaigns of the early 20th century were well-intentioned but misguided. Our science and technology are always more sophisticated than our ability to apply them.

In the same way that poisons used against predators flowed through food chains with unforeseen consequences, our fire suppression efforts have been too successful. The complex interrelationships of fire-dependent plants and animals are unraveling as their habitat diminishes and declines. Where fire exclusion has created abnormally high tree densities, insects and disease are epidemic. And when fuel loads have accumulated beyond historical ranges, fires are destructive rather than restorative. The effects of fire exclusion have been amplified and compounded by most of our logging practices, which have contradicted traditional fire patterns. We've cut the large, dominant trees that normally would have survived fires, and left inferior trees that aren't as well adapted to the site.

Our attempts to replicate fire with logging have typically been limited to clearcuts, reflecting the narrow perspective and industrial bias of conventional forestry. The claim that clearcuts mimic fire isn't entirely valid, as some forest structure remains even after severe fires. Both the standing and fallen dead trees provide food and shelter for microorganisms, insects and birds, and shade for seedlings. They also replenish the soil as they decompose. Smaller amoeba-shaped cuts that retain some standing trees but are open enough to allow seral species to regenerate, are preferable to the indiscriminate use of large rectangular clearcuts.

The introduction of wolves into parts of their former ranges, and a growing tolerance of predators in general, parallels a belated recognition of the value of fire among forest managers. Fire will eventually resume its role as the primary forest predator, whether we want it to or not. We should reintroduce it, or allow fires to burn, when possible, to restore ecosystems suffering from fire exclusion. When this isn't practical, we should replicate fire to the best of our ability with logging that follows the grain of natural patterns.

Thoughtful, carefully executed logging can benefit our forests and our communities. But if the sole purpose of logging is to satisfy harvest quotas or quarterly profits, the methods used are irrelevant, and the best alternative is no action at all. Forests have taken care of themselves for thousands of years;

humanity's clumsy attempts at "management" have proven to be the greatest threat to their health and survival.

In my work, I follow the lead of fire and other forest predators by leaving the dominant tree and cutting the suppressed ones. This improves forest vigor and decreases fire danger. I pay special attention to soil and water, remembering that everything comes from the earth, and is joined by water. By minimizing soil disturbance and maintaining the existing spectrum of plant species of various sizes and ages, I attempt to ensure that habitat values for migrant and resident animals are maintained, even though the general forest density is reduced. Some of the dominant trees I leave are elderly and past their prime; "decadent" in forestry terms. This is often used as a rationale to cut them, but because they're becoming increasing scarce, I choose to protect them, giving them a chance to return to the earth and become fertile soil for their descendants. Attempting to pass off the wholesale liquidation of old growth as forestry is like calling the extermination of the bison herds wildlife management.

It appears that our forests in the northern Rockies have been over-logged, but in light of what fire ecologists are learning about pre-settlement forest densities and fire patterns, it's more often true that they've been poorly logged. While forest densities may have once been lower than they are today, average tree size was larger. The extensive forests and prolific elk herds that our ancestors knew have been whittled into isolated remnants, and the genetic reservoir of mature, dominant individuals is steadily evaporating. In the same way that foresters should advocate forest retention rather than forest removal, wildlife managers should conserve wildlife. But state wildlife departments are funded by legislatures, and the officials charged with making decisions have to temper the recommendations of field biologists with political realities. This doesn't necessarily serve the best interests of wildlife. It seems that some of the regulations are designed to safeguard hunting opportunities rather than preserve genetic quality. For example, in some Montana hunting districts the elk harvest is limited to brow-tined bulls. To me, this is like promoting forest conservation by cutting only large old trees.

Hunters should defend wildlife, rather than hunting, just as loggers should advocate forest preservation, rather than logging. If this statement appears contradictory, it's only because our values and ethics are economically biased. Our terminology reflects this bias: we refer to trees and wildlife as "crops" to be "harvested" by loggers and hunters who are "tools" of resource managers. And when the forests are leveled and the wildlife is gone we create "tree farms" and "game farms." We assign monetary values to trees or elk and reduce them to the status of commodities, hoping to justify their exploitation. But we overlook their true worth. And because we live without reverence, humility and a sense of belonging, we cheapen our own lives as well as the lives of our descendants.

Hunters and loggers have to shed the mantle of victimhood that so many of us have chosen to wear and rise up in defense of the land. If we are more concerned with our standard of living than our quality of life, we've failed to honor our obligations as citizens of the natural community and can merely claim to be exploiters and consumers of its resources. Our measure of success should simply be to leave the land in better condition than we found it.

The demise of wise elk and old trees illustrates our failure to comply with natural laws. If we continue to violate these laws, the future will always be less than the past. But if we honor them, our lives will enrich the earth rather than impoverish it, and the stories we tell our grandchildren will describe what we have given, rather than what we have taken.

Published in Nov/Dec 1998 issue of "Bugle" magazine

Principles And Practices of Wild Forestry

STUDY THE INTERDEPENDENCE of plants, animals, soils, sunlight, water and wind.

Look for the connections between things. Resist the urge to simplify an ecosystem by isolating interconnected elements.

Recognize that the Whole is something more than the sum of its parts.

Acknowledge and embrace the inherent worth of all things.

Admit that our knowledge is ingrained with ignorance. Accept our limited ability to comprehend the mystery, magic and complexity of life.

Challenge the presumption that we can improve upon nature.

Remember that forests have thrived for eons without our assistance. No-action is often the best path.

Industrial Forestry embraces the philosophy of a slaughter-house, where production is paramount, and the taking of life is mindless and disrespectful.

Wild Forestry is practiced with the mind and heart of The Hunter, who takes what he needs with reverence, respect and humility.

Ask the forest what it can provide. Take only what can be removed without harming the forest's integrity and original nature.

Think of the dominant trees as mature bucks, trap-shy coyotes wise old cow elk, or battle-tested boar grizzlies. They carry the past into the future, and the land is poorer without them.

Leave the value on the land. Respect the Elders and they will offer themselves when the time comes.

Think in Forest Time rather than Human Time. Treat the forest as a trust fund that you are obligated to manage for the benefit of future generations of plants, animals and people. Live on the interest, and enrich the principal, through right thinking and good work.

Question capital-intensive forest practices that claim to be sustainable but favor uniformity, simplicity and domestication, and divorce people from the Earth. Increased production at a lower cost is achieved at the expense of the land and its inhabitants.

Support forest practices that keep people on the the ground, employ appropriate technology, promote diversity and honor wildness.

Pay special attention to soil and water, remembering that all things arise from the earth and are joined by water.

Look for reasons to leave trees, rather than cut them.

Work with the Grain, not against it.

Don't be too confident. Be cautious and conservative.

Logging should be a thoughtful process of elimination, in which the decisions become more difficult as the work progresses.

The art of logging lies in knowing when to quit.

Be grateful for the opportunity to work in wild forests and dedicate your life to protecting them.

Presentation to Montana Wilderness Association Annual Convention, regarding alternatives to conventional forestry on public, private and corporate lands. Kalispell, MT. November 1995

Communion

I'VE BEEN A HUNTER for nearly 35 years, and have killed my share of game—cottontails, squirrels, ruffed grouse and whitetails in the Appalachian woodlands of my youth; mule deer and elk in the northern Rockies where I now live. But I've been a dreamer longer than I've been a hunter. I've had powerful dreams at pivotal points in my life; dreams that have given me insight, inspiration and guidance.

For me, dreaming and hunting are essential and satisfying. And they are intertwined, sustaining both body and soul. I often dream of animals as humans; friends I live with in another place and time. Thanks to these dreams, I experience the everyday world through the lens of this other reality. I've dreamed of elk as humans several times, most recently in a camp near the Big Hole Divide.

I'd been hunting there for nearly a week with no luck. Each day the snow was glassy, crunching underfoot until the sun softened it in the late afternoon. The wind was erratic, and always seemed to shift in the wrong direction at crucial moments. The elk were holed up in the most rugged and remote country they could find. I saw some cows and calves but had no cow tag. I tracked some bulls, but never had a decent shot at any of them. Weary and dispirited, I'd reflect on the traces of their passage—splayed hoofprints, the dull rattle of antler on wood, the scent of humus-flecked snow mixed with the sweet tang of crushed lodgepole needles and the potent musk of bull elk. They were like tawny phantoms, always one step or thought ahead of me, as if they were magically shielded from my bullets and strategies. Most of the elk that had been killed in the area had panicked into bullets while fleeing other hunters. Gathered around the evening fire, my hunting partners and I empathized, wishing we could simply count coup on them. But we were hunting for food and had to confront the paradox of killing animals we loved.

This dream came to me one night while a southwest wind swooped down from the Lemhi range, buffeting my frozen tent: I was hunting elk in broken sagebrush country, walking along a sidehill trail, from where I could see the forests of distant mountains. There was an ocean shore below me. A soft wind blew inland, carrying the sound of the surf. I sensed something below me, although it was hidden by the curve of the hill. I froze and crouched, bringing the rifle to my shoulder, expecting an elk to appear.

An adolescent girl stepped into the trail, appearing in the rifle sights. She was bronze skinned, wearing a dress that seemed to be made of cedar bark. I knew she was an Elk Person.

I looked into her innocent, inquisitive eyes, appalled to think I'd nearly killed her. Completely shattered, I cried uncontrollably. On my knees, I apologized and begged her forgiveness. She stroked my head, saying nothing. I knew she forgave me.

Then more Elk People, many generations of them, appeared, seeming to rise up from the earth. They encircled me, dancing and chanting, shapeshifting from elk to human, human to elk. This ceremony honored and blessed our interwoven lives, and showed me that hunting, killing and eating elk was my role in a rite of communion that unites us through flesh, blood and spirit.

Looking through the veil of this dream, I see elk as husbands, wives, sons and grandmothers. Reliving some hunting experiences, I watch death cloud a mother's eye while I kneel beside her in the blood-soaked earth. I cut the heart of someone's daughter out of its translucent sheath and hang it up to cool, slipping the aorta over a spruce limb. I hear the last breath of a grandfather trail off into a morning breeze.

The dream is terrifying and inspiring, but most of all it is humbling. It tells me that life should not be taken unless it is first given, and that this exchange is sacred. And I wonder if we can ever be thankful enough.

December 1997

"Good Hunting"

"Bugle" editor Dan Crockett's column, accompanying "Communion" in the May/June 2000 issue

CAN THERE BE ANYTHING MORE *"WOO-WOO"* than our dreams? We do not understand them. We have no power over them. They come unbidden, leaving us in rapture, in cold, stark terror, in weird befuddlement. We can listen or turn away.

Many of us turn away. Like Scrooge trying to slough off Marley's Ghost as nothing more than a blot of mustard, we dismiss our dreams as nonsense.

Bob Love listens. Maybe that's why we editors have been so squeamish about publishing a slim essay he titled "Communion." We bought this piece more than two years ago and have been sitting on it ever since. The first time this story made the rounds among us, everyone gave it the thumb's-up. We still like it. The sheer force of Love's dream is riveting. The honesty with which he relates the dream and its impact on him is stronger still.

But the last thing we want is to turn readers away from this magazine and, more importantly, from the Elk Foundation. The conservation challenges before us are too big. We need every elk hunter who cares. And there's no shortage of hunters who care about protecting elk country but want nothing to do with articles which try to, as Bob Love puts it, "confront the paradox of killing animals we love."

Many good people, good hunters, just want to read the kind of hunting stories we'd tell each other around a campfire. Never mind all the philosophizing. Over the years we've taken some heat for running "hoodoo-voodoo" stories. So Love's story stayed down in the dark water we call "the well." Eventually, though, that came to seem a tad cowardly. When a lifelong hunter has the courage to recount a dream which rocked his foundations, keeping his story in perpetual limbo doesn't seem like an adequate response.

I enjoy a good straight-up hunting story as much as anyone (check out "Hard Luck," "The Beaver Dam Incident," and "Showdown on the Firing Line" for a start on this issue). But I like mysteries as well.

Is there any hunter who hasn't *"felt"* the presence of a bull or buck before their eyes, ears or nose detected it? Haven't we all known the prickle of being watched, and turned to find bird or beast gazing intently upon us?

What is that thing which passes between creature and person at such moments? It's a mystery to me, and a delightful one at that. I don't want to know the answer any more than I want to know why I fell in love with a particular woman or river. I want the feeling itself, not the rationale behind it.

Few of us would spend most of the night tossing as if on a rotisserie, then set forth before dawn with a rifle or bow in hand if we already knew what was going to happen. It's the chance to rub elbows with fate, the *"possibility"* of an encounter, that keeps the drumroll pounding in our hearts.

Hunting well assumes mastering the skills of reading sign, spotting, stalking, shooting. It implies learning all you can about your quarry and the country where it lives. For me, though, none of these things replace intuition. Sure it's great to have a game plan, but if you feel yourself tugged toward a different basin, do not resist. Go there.

Poet and novelist (and hunter) Jim Harrison wrote "Perhaps it takes a culture as slippery and venal as our own to discount the dream life that was so vital to people for 30,000 years."

Given that backdrop of 300 centuries, it might be wise to view dreams as messengers arriving from strange countries. Shall we kill them because we don't understand them?

How often do any of us truly listen to our dreams and our hunches, let alone heed them? Neurologists conclude that most of us use less than 10 percent of our brains. It doesn't seem too far-fetched to imagine that dreams and intuitions arise from the nine-tenths of our brain which remains unknown to us. Maybe they're just the cartoons, horror flicks and static of our subconscious. Perhaps they are metaphors for how we might better conduct our lives.

Those who detest touchy-feely stories may want to give Bob Love's story a miss. On the other hand, it might be worth considering how you'd feel if his dream had visited you. As that notorious softy Ernest Hemmingway once wrote, "It is awfully easy to be hardboiled about everything in the daytime, but at night it is another thing."

The Forests of Lookout Ridge

THE ORIGINAL TITLE OF THIS REPORT was "Forest Management on Lookout Ridge." I changed it because the phrase "forest management" implies that we are making demands of the forest, when we should be asking what it's able to provide, and still be healthy. It also assumes that trees, like wheat or corn, need to be tended by humans. But applying agriculture models and language to natural systems like forests reduces their resources to commodities; trees become logs, which are sawn into lumber, which speculators trade to turn a profit. This system powers monetary economies at the expense of natural economies and ecologies. But when forest ecosystems are impaired or destroyed, the economies that rely on them also collapse.

It's juvenile, and dangerous, to assume that forests need us more than we need them; forests have "managed" themselves for millions of years, without our help. Plants were the earliest life forms on the planet. From their perspective, everything, including humans, is merely compost. The interrelationships between plant communities and animals are ancient. They are ingrained in us as well but are beyond our rational comprehension. If we see ourselves as part of the forest, rather than separate from it (in charge of it) we interact with it cautiously, and respectfully. Earlier cultures knew this, and some of their traditions survived into modern times. For example, here in the Flathead, the Kutenai Indians used to strip bark from elderly Ponderosa pine in the spring to harvest the cambium, which was dried and used as a sweetener. This work was done by committee. A group of men selected the tree and offered gifts and apologies to it. Then each man took a turn with the axe. That way, if the spirit of the tree was offended for some reason, any retribution would be spread among the group instead of being inflicted on one person.

Traces of this wisdom still exist in our DNA, but we discount it. When I was a timber faller working in the industrial forestry world, a co-worker and I were considering how to clearcut a basin that sheltered about 30 log truck loads of 500-year-old spruce trees. The forest felt healthy to me, and the idea of razing it made me uneasy. I said, "I don't think we should be logging here." He said, "Oh maybe we should do this first," and pantomimed an Indian, dancing around and chanting, like he was praying to the trees. I said, "That's a good start, but we still shouldn't do it." We cut those trees because that was our trade and we had families to feed. But that didn't make it any easier for me to accept. In a sense, we couldn't afford to leave the place alone. I hope we eventually learn that we can't afford to cut places like this either.

After a twenty-year career as a production timber faller I decided to use my skills to improve forests rather than remove them. As a logger, this seemed eminently sensible, and necessary. It turned out that there were plenty of opportunities to use this approach. At the very least, private forests in our region are suffering from fire-exclusion and need to be thinned. Most of them have also been neglected, after being repeatedly traumatized by loggers, and need some thoughtful attention to help them heal. This healing, like surgery, often requires cutting. But this cutting is closer to sculpture, paring away the excess, shaping forests so that, over time, they resemble those that existed prior to white settlement. But this will require periodic human intervention (logging or prescribed fire) working with, not against, the Grain of natural patterns. The work will have to be done on Forest Time, by several generations of humans, most of whom won't live to see the end result. This may seem like a Utopian dream, but I prefer it to the dream that deludes our consumer-driven society into believing that we can disregard traditional ecologic patterns with impunity. That dream is a fantasy, and a nightmare.

Forests, like everything in the universe, are dynamic. At the microscopic level, complex fungal interactions cycle nutrients through air, water, soil and plants. This is the foundation of the food chain; iconic species like grizzly bears and elk wouldn't exist if some nearly invisible, mostly unknown creatures weren't diligently creating soil from rock and wood. Without their help, we wouldn't be here either.

Fire is the most dramatic and sudden force of change in our ecosystem. The intensity and frequency of fire varies, according to terrain and slope aspect; steep slopes burn faster than flat ground, and wetter, cooler north slopes are less fire-prone than drier south slopes. Wind-driven fires break all the rules and burn through all forest types and terrains. There are three basic fire regimes in northwest Montana, distinguished mostly by fire intervals (average years between fires) and fire behavior.

Low-intensity fires on the valley floors burned on 20–50-year intervals, through stands of Western larch, Douglas fir and Ponderosa pine. These thick-barked species tolerate fire and welcome it; their seeds germinate best in mineral soil exposed by fires. These fires typically killed understory trees, removing the competition from the larger overstory. They also consumed excessive duff, and rejuvenated shrubs, forbs and grasses. The ancestors of our indigenous neighbors set them deliberately to improve game habitat and berry production. These fires, like the people who relied on them for sustenance, can't roam freely anymore.

Mixed-severity fires burned on the mountain slopes between the valley floor and the subalpine zone. They burned on a 40–100-year cycle. The forests on these slopes are mixed conifer stands, composed of larch, Douglas fir, Ponderosa pine in the lower and drier sites, Lodgepole pine, White pine, Western cedar and Grand fir in the higher and wetter sites. In windy conditions these fires climb into the forest canopy and cover a lot of country. In calm weather they might stay on the forest floor, killing some larger trees and sparing others. The randomness of these fires creates a variety of species, age classes and density. This is the predominant fire regime on Lookout Ridge, where its effects are most noticeable on the western, southwestern, southern, southeastern exposures, and less so on the northeast slope. Most of the trees are about 100 years old, but I've found some Douglas firs below the house site that are about 300 years old, and have survived three fires, at roughly 100-year intervals. The last significant fire here was in 1919, so, from a historical perspective, the southern/western slopes of Lookout Ridge are due for another one.

Another fire regime, classified as stand-replacement, is the most catastrophic, at least from a human perspective. These fires usually burn in the alpine zone, below timberline, in Engelmann spruce, Subalpine fir and Whitebark pine stands. Pure Lodgepole pine stands in the lower alpine zone are also consumed and regenerated by stand-replacement fires. These fire intervals range from 200-500 years. The Old Growth microsite in the northern part of the property is in this fire regime, as evidenced by the age of the trees. I sampled a larch here that was killed in the last fire (1910 or 1919) that didn't show any previous fire scars. It was roughly 400 years old at that time.

Human activity is another driver of forest dynamics. It can be benign—hunter gatherers used forests lightly, maybe because fire was the only technology they had to alter them. It can be beneficial—modern equipment can be used to thin forests to promote health and decrease fire danger. Or it can be detrimental, to wantonly extract trees as quickly and cheaply as possible. But intention is more important than the technology that is used: after all, most of the deforestation that has occurred in the course of human history was accomplished with hand labor and livestock.

For discussion purposes I've identified and named several distinct areas on the Lookout Ridge property. They each have unique features, qualities and histories. I describe them separately, but they are interconnected, because the boundaries between them are fluid and permeable.

Old Growth

This is a small canyon in the northwest corner of Lookout Ridge with a northern aspect, forming a tributary of Haskill Creek. The forest is composed of Grand fir, Western hemlock, Western red cedar, Western larch, Douglas fir and Subalpine fir. These are the oldest trees on the property. Wildfires here are infrequent, typically on a cycle of 300 to 500 years, due to shade, moisture and cool temperatures. Some of the Grand fir and hemlock have fire scars, from 1919, on the uphill side. Since these thin-barked species don't survive hot fires, this tells me that the fire crested on the ridgeline and crawled around on the forest floor for the most part. There are old skid trails and roads which were used to log fire-killed larch snags for cordwood in the winter, evidenced by numerous waist-high stumps. No significant logging has been done here. Although the trees are large, most of them are rotten.

The timber industry refers to these old growth stands as over-mature or decadent, and typically cuts them to get a new forest growing. Old growth has become scarcer, and more ecologically valuable. The remnant stands are predominantly in remote, steep terrain in the headwaters of watersheds like Haskill Basin, where they stabilize fragile soils and nurture stream flows. Growth rates and nutrient cycling are slower in old growth stands than they are in younger forests on more favorable sites. Besides having ecological value, old growth stands have spiritual values, which aren't easily defined with words. Being among ancient trees gives you a different sense of time. Maybe that's why so many of us are drawn to them and feel comfortable among them.

These places are primeval sanctuaries that would have evoked similar emotions in the hearts of our most distant ancestors. In light of their scarcity there has been more resistance to cutting old growth, and more emphasis on protecting existing stands. Old growth on private land is especially rare. Over the course of my 45-year career I've come across some ancient trees on private land, but they're always lone individuals, spared from the saw because they were rotten. I've never seen an extensive, fairly intact stand like this on private land.

Logging isn't a threat to these trees, but climate change is. In the past few years we have had several catastrophic wind events, that in my opinion, are related to climate change. These trees are relatively safe from high winds because they are sheltered in a deep draw. Climate change is also affecting fire behavior, spawning larger, more frequent and intense fires, so this stand is more susceptible to fire than it has been historically. A wind-driven crown fire could cross the ridge and flow into the crowns of these trees as well. Other potential ignition sources are lightning, or fires started by recreationists on the Whitefish Trail, north of the property boundary.

Northeast Slope

This area lies between the ridgeline above the pond site and the eastern property line.

The Old Growth area is the northern boundary. The southern boundary is the old Stoltze road that drops down over the hill northeast of the main house site. It has the same conifer species as the Old Growth area, but there are fewer hemlock. The overstory trees are somewhat younger than those in the Old Growth area, probably because there have been more frequent fires. This moderately steep terrain has been extensively logged by Stoltze. There are a few larger Doug firs, cedars and Grand firs scattered among brush fields that have grown up in the aftermath of the logging. The Grand firs and cedars were left because they are rotten; the large Douglas firs were left for some inexplicable reason. Most of the older larch were cut, unless they were rotten. There is good regeneration of all species. This slope is somewhat moister and less fire-prone than the southern/western aspects of the property, so an old growth stand could eventually grow here again. In 2019 I did some logging on the knob above the southern boundary, removing dead/ dying/rotten Grand firs that were maimed during Stoltze's logging operations. Fortunately, I found some younger Doug fir and larch that I was able to leave. Dense brush and abundant browse provide good food and security for deer, moose, elk, snowshoe hares, songbirds, grouse and bears. This slope is also a likely spot for bear dens.

Southeast Slope Below Main House

This is a small basin that is a transition zone between the moist, sheltered northern aspects of the property and the drier, more exposed southwest/western slopes. At various times in the past Stolze removed the larger, more valuable Doug fir, larch and cedar, leaving scraggly cedar thickets in their wake. This is one of the first areas we worked in last summer (2019). We did the best we could with the cedar stands, although there wasn't much to work with. We also did some extensive thinning in regenerating sapling stands, favoring the vigorous larch and Doug fir.

South Slope Below Main House

This area is a living example of how fire, fire suppression and extractive forestry have shaped the forests in our region. The forest here was shaped by mixed-severity fires. Unlike even-aged forests composed of one species, these forests are more resilient to insects and disease than forests composed of even-aged trees of the same species. They also provide habitat for a wider variety of wildlife species than even-aged monocultures.

Without occasional fires the ecological quality of these forests declines; they become unnaturally dense, so that when and if they burn, the fires are more catastrophic than helpful. Fire suppression was institutionalized by bureaucracies in the early twentieth century, especially here in northwest Montana. At the same time, timber companies were cutting ancient trees that were fire-dependent, and fire-tolerant. Consequently, ecological patterns and inter-relationships that co-evolved over thousands of years were disrupted and thwarted in a few decades.

Forests that were historically composed of large, widely spaced, fire tolerant species converted by default into thickets of smaller, more volatile species. As I said, this forest illustrates the story: First, there hasn't been any significant fire here since 1919. Second, it's been logged about three times, and each entry has left it further devalued; the last logging operation removed most of the dominant Douglas fir and larch and left rotten Grand fir.

If a fire had burned on this slope 50 years ago there would be some younger fir and larch, more older larch and Doug fir than there are currently, and fewer Grand fir. If a fire came through here now there wouldn't be much left, thanks to the unnaturally high numbers of Grand fir, one of the most flammable species in the forest. The logging also compacted and displaced soils, damaged many residual trees and their root systems, and probably stimulated the spread of endemic root disease. Climate change is also helping to unravel this forest. Grand firs in northwest Montana are living on the extreme eastern edge of their range; they prefer the milder, moister maritime habitats to our west, and can't tolerate the drier, warmer weather we've experienced lately. If current trends continue, Grand fir in our region will only exist in isolated microsites. Complicating matters further, the main house is being built on the summit of this slope. In the event of a fire, this is like building it on top of a chimney, especially if nothing is done to reduce the fuel loading. But this isn't as simple as it sounds, especially when the area is in the viewshed of the house, and aesthetic concerns are paramount.

One option is to use machinery to cut the Grand fir and leave the larger Doug fir, taking care to protect the larch and Doug fir regeneration in the process. Another is to do this incrementally, taking only dead and ailing Grand fir as needed. The problem with this approach is that you inevitably damage some of the regeneration that infills the openings over time. I did some of this in 2019 but didn't get too close to the house site. The work can be done manually, but it's hard to remove or burn large chunks of wood, and maybe even harder to find people who will do it.

Walking through this area recently I noticed some large Grand fir that had been blown down in a windstorm this spring. Fir engraver beetles will lay eggs in these trees in the next few weeks, and if the trees aren't removed, beetles will emerge from them next year and kill standing green Grand firs. Further down the slope, along the southern property line, Douglas fir beetles are currently laying eggs in trees that were windthrown in the same storm. We created access to this area last week, and I've cleaned up most of the windfalls. I'm also taking the dead and dying Grand fir while I'm there. Consequently, this area is more open than the upper slope. This open space may slow down any fire that emerges from the Iron Horse development. It's not visible from the house, and it may be a good idea to extend this buffer zone northward along the property line.

Southwest Slope Below Main House

This slope is extremely steep and densely forested, primarily with Douglas fir. Because of the steep slope it's never been logged. These trees have been growing tightly since they regenerated after the 1919 fire. The crowns are spare and narrow, indicating that the stand is thinning itself. There are some older larch and Doug fir (+/-300 yrs.) that survived the fire. There are some recent blowdowns that should be removed to inhibit future beetle attacks. Some thinning work, either manual or mechanical (if there's access), could be done to decrease fuels.

Southwest Slope Below West Ridge

The water tower marks the southern tip of this area, and a landmark named Poppy's Peak on the trail map marks the northern boundary. This forest, like the slope below the house, has been shaped by fire. I first worked here in the late 90's, for various landowners who owned small tracts. I returned in 2008, working for Brian Fimian, who bought these tracts and included them in the Lookout Ridge subdivision. The end result was similar to the forest you see on your right, just past the shop, as you drive along the main road. Visually, my work replicated the effects of mixed-severity fires; species, ages and density are diverse, and the plant communities on the forest floor are intact. Some foresters claim that this kind of mechanical treatment is a substitute for fire, but I don't agree; when it comes to nutrient cycling, which contributes to soil health, and ultimately forest health, there is no substitute for fire. In the 1970s the Forest Service grudgingly accepted this ecological fact; now they use prescribed fire to reduce fuels, to improve big game habitat. They also allow some fires in the backcountry to burn. In the future we may learn how to use fire in the urban interface; until then we'll have to reduce fuels mechanically.

The logging that was done here in early 2019, before I was brought into the current project in July, is typical of most of the work that's being done on Forest Service, Montana DNRC lands and private industrial lands. Although industry standards for soil compaction, residual stand damage and visual appearance are higher than they were in the past, the focus is still more on extraction than stewardship. This work is acceptable to commodity-driven foresters, but too harsh for most private owners. Fortunately, this is one of the most productive and resilient forests on the property, and it will heal quickly.

This forest, like the slope below the house, has been shaped by fire, but unlike that slope, the soil and vegetation weren't displaced by heavy-handed logging, at least when I first worked there in the late 90s. Other than clearcutting the horse pasture, and doing some preliminary clearing for the equestrian facility, I didn't do much here in 2019. I spent about a week this year cutting and removing windthrown Douglas firs, from above the lower gate to below the horse pasture. This slope and the ridgeline at the summit is premium winter range for whitetails, mule deer and elk.

When I worked here 25 years ago there was more game than there is now. It was about that time that wolves drifted into the country. Besides wolves, coyotes and mountain lions hunted on the winter range, and bears killed deer fawns and elk calves in the spring. Although predators get most of the blame for decimating ungulate populations, habitat decline (from fire suppression), displacement (from residential development and recreational activity), and abnormal weather (due to climate change) are more pernicious threats to big game. The forest in this area also yields reliable, heavy crops of huckleberries, an invaluable local resource that we too often take for granted.

West-Northwest Slope Below Shop and the Caretaker's House

This is the steepest terrain on the property, and some of the most densely forested, with Doug fir along the boundary and cedar thickets above the Lookout Loop Road. A fire here in dry and windy conditions would be nearly impossible to contain. Some prudent thinning in the Doug fir below the road could improve the health of the stand, but won't make it fireproof, due to the extreme slope. With that in mind, we should aggressively thin the cedar thickets above the road to create a fuelbreak in more moderate terrain. We should also leave a significant screen of forest along the Big Mountain Road. The forest around the shop and caretaker's residence should be watched closely over the next few years. Construction activities and excavation damaged many trees, making them attractive to beetles that incubated in the green logs that were left lying around. Beetle-hit trees should be removed before the larvae hatch and emerge the next year. Pheromone packets can deter Douglas fir beetles and should be used on the property wherever large Doug firs are stressed or windthrown. I recommended this to Spencer, and Forestoration crews are planning to do this soon.

Fringe Forest Around the Pond

This "doghair" forest is composed of cedar thickets that grew in the wake of the 1919 fire. These spindly trees are malnourished and deprived of sunlight because they grew too densely. The forest on the eastern ridgeline is a tangle of cedar and Grand fir thickets. Stoltze did some haphazard logging in places that mangled many of the scraggly trees. West of the pond, I did some thinning and fuel reduction work in 2008, working with Reid Sabin's hand crews. This forest is more visually appealing than the one on the eastern ridge, but it is still stagnant. If it belonged to me I would make small irregular openings, burn the slash in them and plant some larch if they didn't regenerate naturally. Doing this over time would gradually create more diversity without being too noticeable. There are a few survivors of previous fires scattered throughout these fringe forests, as well some larch, Doug firs, Lodgepole pines and Grand firs that germinated after the fire. The Lodgepoles and Grand firs are failing, naturally fading from the stand as they reach the end of their lives. The larch and Doug fir are vigorous at this point, but they will weaken if the thickets encroaching on them aren't removed. The cedar on the edge of the pond site is turning brown because it was suddenly exposed to the sun, after living in the shade of a dense forest for a century. This is called sun scalding. It may also kill other shade tolerant species like hemlock, spruce and Grand fir, as well as seral species like larch and Lodgepole, in some circumstances. There is no cure for sun scalding, but it can be ameliorated, and sometimes prevented, if trees growing in these conditions are gradually exposed to direct sunlight by cautiously thinning them over time.

Wetland

The pond site, before it was cleared, was an extension of this wetland, a riparian forest composed of spruce, cedar, cotton-wood and birch. Moose wintered in it and bears came here in the spring to feed on cottonwood buds; I know this because I've watched them doing it. The wetland and the surrounding forest is still valuable habitat, even though it's a fragment of what was originally there.

The cedars in the small basin south of the wetland are healthy because they're living in a hospitable micro-site. This is a multi-aged forest composed of young, middle-aged and older trees. The older ones are fire scarred. I aged one tree that was about 200 years old, with no apparent fire scars.

Main Road

Dead or dying trees that could fall into the road should be removed. Most of these are Grand firs, north of the Pond Site Road. The dense Douglas fir forest on the slope above the wetland could be thinned, or not. In any case, it's thinning itself.

Basic Management Philosophy

Encourage diversity in species, ages and forest density. To help a forest move in the direction it wants to go you need to become familiar with the spirits who live there, who make that place original and unique. Sit down. Be quiet. Watch. Listen. If you think you should intervene by cutting or burning, temper the work with patience, and caution. Don't follow a blanket prescription when it comes to tree selection or spacing. Leave some places alone! Accept chaos, randomness, and anarchy, and your work will look natural.

Specific Suggestions

Larch, Douglas fir and cedar grow in every part of the property, on all aspects, in every habitat type and fire regime. This tells me that they are the major climax forest species. Favor them generally, but not to the exclusion of other species. Hemlock is also a climax species here, as indicated by its presence in the Old Growth area. Conditions aren't suitable for it now, but it will appear as the forest matures and the canopy closes. Grand fir also grows in the Old Growth area and will be part of the climax forest in some places, but not on southern and western aspects. Grand fir in these places will continue to die because of climate change, creating hazardous fuel levels. We should aggressively cut Grand fir, especially the regenerating thickets, which are encroaching on Douglas fir and larch. Lastly, declare war on weeds!

Summary

When I offered to write this report I assumed I could do it in a couple of evenings. It seemed simple: present some basic concepts and information about our region's forests and show how they apply to Lookout Ridge in particular. But the more I wrote, the more I found to write about. I've worked on it for a few days, and could carry on for a few more, exploring topics like wildlife, wildlife habitat, deciduous trees, and understory plants. As it is, I hope it's helpful to people who aren't familiar with our forests, and to those who will be working on Lookout Ridge in the future. Questions, comments and suggestions are welcome.

Bob Love, *Confluence Timber Company*
Columbia Falls MT, June 30, 2020

The Loggers

I'VE WORKED AS A LOGGER in the forests of northwest Montana for nearly twenty-five years. In the early part of my career I was a timber faller for a large company, cutting for their high-lead yarders on national forest timber sales. When that outfit folded in the mid-1980s, I hired on with an independent contractor who did similar work, but on smaller sales. As the flow of federal timber declined in the late 1980s, he decided to work exclusively for Plum Creek Timber, on its land.

At that time Plum Creek was "liquidating its assets" (cutting the best and leaving the rest) in order to satisfy corporate debts and bolster quarterly profit reports. As I grew increasingly dissatisfied with this so-called forestry, I publicly voiced my opposition to it, mostly in letters to local and regional papers. Even though many of my fellow loggers privately agreed with me, few of them were willing to bite the hand that fed them. As I became more estranged from the logging community and frustrated with my inability to affect the system, I chose to make some career changes.

While my livelihood depended on sustainable forest management, I was being paid to feed the insatiable appetites of sawmills. This obviously didn't serve the best interests of the land, my family, or my community. I decided to use my skills to benefit the land or find another trade. I had to shift my priorities from forest removal to forest retention. Since this contradicted what was happening on industrial and public lands, the only option left to me was to become an independent contractor for private nonindustrial forest owners. I started down this road eight years ago.

At the same time I openly challenged conventional forestry practices, I became familiar with some local environmentalists; we were attending many of the same hearings, workshops and field tours. The underlying assumption of these affairs was that loggers and environmentalists disagreed on everything, and all the players stuck to the script. The deeper the adversaries dug in their heels, the more certain the Forest Service was that resolution was impossible.

I realized that if either side "won," we would all lose and sensed that reasonable people could find some common ground if a few of us were willing to drop our defenses and step out of the trenches. Acting on this intuition, I called Steve Thompson of the Montana Wilderness Association. We organized some tours where loggers and MWA members looked at both good and bad forestry, without Forest Service intervention.

We found plenty to argue about, but without the contrived contentiousness that normally framed our meetings, we got to know one another better. As we shared rides, lunches, opinions and stories, we began to see one another as neighbors rather than members of special-interest groups. For the first time, loggers and environmentalists approached the Forest Service with a unified front and offered a cohesive vision for the future. Essentially, we agreed that the timber frontier was closed, and that we had to learn to live within limits. The Forest Service didn't know what to make of this. Although some employees were supportive, we encountered institutional resistance, and the true believers in the environmental and logging communities regarded us as traitors.

This all happened more than a decade ago. Some of the relationships formed during that time deepened into friendships, while some friendships that existed prior to that period disintegrated. At any rate, our voluntary cease-fire encouraged more thoughtful, civil discussions about public forest issues, and led to the creation of the Flathead Forestry Project. FFP is an ad hoc group dedicated to restoring trust among the timber industry, conservationists, and the Forest Service by promoting small timber sales and stewardship projects in our national forests. The group has been meeting for eight years and has had some influence on Forest Service policy, despite bureaucratic inertia and the active resistance of some environmental organizations and industrial trade groups.

A key principle that emerged from those initial conversations, and still guides the FFP, is that we don't have to enter roadless areas to find logs. There's plenty of work to do in the roaded frontcountry, where we've consistently eaten dessert before cleaning our plate. I recall several Forest Service tours of proposed timber sales where we drove past forty miles of salvage, thinning, fuel-reduction and restoration work, only to arrive at an alpine basin at the end of a road where nobody thought we should be working anyway. But instead of addressing the challenging and complex issues associated with previously managed forests, we have chosen to reckon damages, assign blame and antagonize one another, to the detriment of the land and our communities. The failure of the Clinton-era debate about roadless area management was that it distracted us from more urgent deliberations about the treatment of roaded areas.

In a global context, our nation is like a gated community. We may be the only people in the world who can afford to spend so much time and energy bickering about the fate of wildlands. Our circumstance is both tragic and fortunate. Tragic, in that our ability to preserve backcountry while we neglect the stewardship of our frontcountry has been facilitated by unsustainable resource extraction from other places. Fortunate, in that the ecosystems of our national forests are resilient and relatively intact. I believe our thoughtful interaction with these landscapes is warranted and desirable, and the responsible thing to do.

I was at a party a few years ago when a woman approached me and said she'd heard I was "quite a conservationist." When I said that I tried to be, she remarked, "That's good, because I'm not on the loggers' side at all." When I told her I worked in the woods, she seemed more perplexed than embarrassed, and bolted away without saying a word. Her reaction reflects a political climate that stifles independent thinking, provokes animosity between people who should be allies, and strengthens the corporate influence on public resource issues. Although it's widely assumed that most loggers aren't conservationists, I know many who are, and I believe we all should be.

As a logger, I support timber management in our national forests. As a hunter and backcountry wanderer, I value wilderness and roadless areas. We can and should have both. To achieve this balance we need to pay attention, proceed cautiously, and learn to ask the land what it can provide, rather than make demands of it. Ideally, the forestry we practice in our national forests should honor the spirit—the wildness—of the land. It should work in concert with natural cycles and patterns, respectfully harvesting the forests' interest rather than plundering their capital, attuning local economies to the land's productive capacity. Finally, this forestry should be more labor- than capital-intensive, and more manual than mechanical, so that our national forests would provide opportunities for young people to learn the land and spend their lives caring for it. In this way, our public forests would serve as sanctuaries for the skills and wisdom that are discounted in industrial forests.

When I compare my utopian vision with reality, I'm not optimistic. The polarization in our communities is increasing. The Forest Service is still being whip-sawed between environmental and industrial lobbyists who have no affinity with rural communities and landscapes. As logging becomes more mechanized, foresters design timber sales to match the machinery, and the site-sensitive projects suited for small logging outfits and restoration specialists fall through the planning cracks. And I don't see many young people seeking a career in the woods.

But I'm going to keep swimming against the current—I'm convinced there are some deep pools upstream. And, paraphrasing Robert Frost, I'd like you to come, too.

Published in the "Roadless Yaak Anthology," 2002

Bugs

RESIDENTS OF THE BITTERROOT LAKE area may have noticed more dead and dying trees in the local forests lately. Mature Douglas firs and Lodgepole pines have been girdled by Fir and Pine beetles, while trees of all species and age classes have been defoliated by Spruce budworms and Tussock moths. Although the prevailing popular opinion is that "bugs" are the primary cause of forest mortality, the truth is that they're attracted to and kill trees which are stressed by age, root disease, drought, fire or excessive competition.

Most of the time, this activity isn't widespread or apparent; the insects are quietly doing their part to thin the forest, and vigorous trees will survive occasional attacks. Epidemic outbreaks and widespread mortality usually occur in forests that are mature, but decadent (in the sense that most of the trees aren't growing appreciably). These forests are relatively stable as long as there is sufficient water, but a prolonged drought may weaken them, making them more attractive and susceptible to beetles and defoliators. Pure stands of elderly lodgepole and spruce are especially susceptible to beetle epidemics, just as they are to stand-replacing fires. In the past few years Douglas fir beetles have run rampant in some drier forests in central Montana, leaving a landscape of dead, red trees in their wake. The popular opinion seems to be that the beetles are the problem, but the actual problem is that there are too many Douglas firs; the tree population has exceeded the productive capacity of the land, and the beetles are doing their part to thin the forest.

Photographs taken around Montana in the early 20th century show that in most cases, the forests were generally more open then than they are today; my observations and intuitions lead me to believe that prior to European settlement, the low-elevation forests in northwest Montana were composed of fewer, larger, older trees. This was especially true in areas like Bitterroot Lake, where ground fires periodically removed the younger understory from the dominant canopy of fire-resistant Ponderosa pine, Western larch and Douglas fir. For the most part, stumps are the only evidence that this forest type existed; the size and spacing of these stumps reveals the average tree size and the forest density at the time the trees were cut. During the 20th century, logging has reduced the average tree diameter while fire suppression has increased the average forest density, leaving our forests more susceptible to fire, drought and insects.

Although we seem to have emerged from a dry period, the climate is warming and the seasonal patterns are shifting and erratic. We still get heavy June rains, but our summers have been hotter than normal, so trees, soils, woody debris and understory plants are drying faster and earlier, making the forest more fire prone. Thanks to longer, warmer summers, there are often multiple beetle hatches, where traditionally there was only one. Warmer winters are also working to the insects' advantage; prolonged cold snaps will dampen or extinguish beetle outbreaks, but sub-zero weather has become increasingly rare. If these climatic trends continue we can expect more beetle outbreaks as well as hotter, larger wildfires, and sparser forests than we're accustomed to.

The forest will thin itself one way or another, but landowners can make the process less traumatic by giving their trees more elbow room, especially in stands of younger and middle-aged trees. Thinning these stands early, and periodically into the future, keeps them vigorous and resilient. I've noticed that thinned stands of young trees have suffered less damage from budworms than unthinned thickets. Older trees are less responsive but will often get a new lease on life if they're given some space. Thinning will also reduce fire danger, but it's not necessary to make your forest resemble a cornfield; leaving some thickets and clumps of trees makes the woods more wildlife-friendly, and aesthetically appealing. It's also not advisable to glean every stick from the forest floor or cut every dead tree; rotting logs, stumps and snags harbor microbes, insects, birds and small mammals that prey on beetles and budworms. The remnant old-growth larch trees scattered around Bitterroot Lake weren't logged off because they were too rotten to yield lumber. Although they're economically worthless, they have incredible ecologic value, and should be protected.

At the landscape level, maintaining habitat for insect predators and thinning are the only practical ways to limit insect damage to the forest. In residential settings, selected trees can be invigorated with fertilizer and protected from insects with chemicals or hormones. There are some local arborists who specialize in these treatments. Most homeowners and arborists are concerned with saving larger, older trees. This is understandable, but will prove to be a poor investment if seedlings and saplings aren't diligently thinned. Service foresters from Montana DNRC can provide free technical assistance with insect control and thinning treatments.

Although insects that kill trees are still referred to as "pests," this is only true of invasive species, which we have unwittingly spread via our global trade networks. Native insects are essential to maintaining healthy forest ecosystems in ways we are only beginning to understand.

Forests in northwest Montana thrived for thousands of years despite the presence of "destructive forest pests," and without the help of foresters. In light of the damage inflicted on our region's forests in one century, I'd say that humans are a greater threat to trees than insects ever were. Pine beetles and Spruce budworms have been managing the forest longer, in a more sustainable fashion, than we have. We should learn to live with them, and begin to learn from them.

Written for the Bitterroot Lake Homeowner's Association,.
February 2013

Thirty-Quart Bucks and Other Measures of Success

"The old man said hunting wasn't so much what you brought back in your bag, but what you'd invested in it, if you were content to take a small return on your investment."
Robert Ruark, "The Old Man and the Boy"

FOLLOWING EACH BIG GAME SEASON here in Montana, the Department of Fish, Wildlife and Parks publishes hunter success rates based on information gathered at game check stations. Success is determined simply by whether or not a hunter killed an animal. On the average, fewer than 10 percent of the hunters surveyed are successful on that basis. Even though most of us get skunked most of the time, we keep hunting. Like the old man in Ruark's book, we evidently find some value in fruitless days.

Although concepts of success vary according to our goals and expectations, we often use numbers to validate it, and the way we apply the numbers reveals our needs and biases. Game managers record harvest numbers, then appraise them within a context of population trends and the land's carrying capacity. While many hunters measure success by the standards of the Boone and Crockett record books, a friend of mine—who can accurately estimate, in the field, how many jars of canned meat any deer will yield—evaluates his hunting season by the deflection of his pantry shelves: his 30-quart whitetail doe is equivalent to the trophy hunter's 190-inch buck.

But numbers don't really measure success. Statistically, the hunter who kills an animal is successful, while a hunter who forgoes a chancy shot and resigns himself to eating track stew is tallied in the "unsuccessful" column. Regarding him as a failure is akin to implying that Mother Teresa wasted her life because she didn't amass a fortune.

Seasoned hunters know that failure leads to success. A few seasons back while I was exploring some new elk hunting territory, I hunted hard, and fruitlessly, for two weeks. I was discouraged, but not surprised; an analysis of my elk-hunting career would yield statistics like one elk per 200 miles of walking (where elk walk), or one elk quarter per 500 windfalls crossed (nothing under knee-high counts). The following year I returned to the area and killed a fat cow before noon of the first day I went out. Someone in camp said I sure was lucky. I didn't disagree, but two thoughts occurred to me: first, that the boot leather, brainpower, Snickers bars and jerky I'd invested the previous season hadn't hurt my chances any; and second, that if it was considered lucky to kill one elk per 15 hunting days, I didn't want to experience hardship.

Ardent elk hunters define success by their own eccentric standards. I was so lucky once that I got to backpack an elk out an open trail, downhill all the way to the pickup. And to top it off, I only had to make four six-mile round trips! One diehard in our camp, who has had a chronic case of elk fever for over 60 years, thinks he's beaten the odds if he only polishes off two magnum bottles of Ibuprofen per season. Appropriately enough, this zealot is the namesake of a certain "Idiot's Basin" in the Middle Fork of the Flathead River.

If we judged our hunting success solely by conventional standards of return on investment, we'd throw in the towel and buy our meat. Killing and caring for wild meat can be arduous and time-consuming, but it yields rewards that can't be measured monetarily; the meat is toxin-free, and hunting (non-motorized) is a healthy lifestyle.

Plus, we have good stories to tell, and the freedom to set our own standards of accomplishment.

Killing efficiently is only one facet of hunting competently. The adage that "the work starts when you pull the trigger" is at best half-true. Learning to shoot isn't very difficult. But learning to hunt is a life-long process that a true hunter never tires of. As a greenhorn I focused mostly on my prey, assuming this was the key to success. Fortunately, my bloodlust was always tempered by the enjoyment of being in the woods. Even though I usually got skunked, I was learning the ecological basics of the Appalachian woodlands where I grew up: Cottontails bedded where blackberry thickets encroached into uncut timothy,

Ruffed grouse roosted in the grapevines near the sandstone quarry, Fox squirrels preferred to nest in White oaks next to corn fields and defended their territory from gray squirrels who lived in beech groves further back in the woods. It didn't take much to sidetrack me--a fox track, an owl pellet, a buck rub, a Redtail nest, a shed Blacksnake skin, or a Ringneck's breast feather could make me lose my hunting-focus. But while I was hunting poorly, I was actually becoming a better hunter; I was sub-consciously assembling these seemingly separate, insignificant things into a picture of the local landscape, until the connections between them became apparent, and so numerous that I eventually realized they were infinite.

This training helped me when I moved from western Pennsylvania to northwest Montana in the early 1970s. In order to hunt well in this new territory, I had to learn its unique ecologic interconnections, as well as the annual events which attend autumn's passage into winter: In a draw above Hallowatt Creek, grizzly bears preparing for hibernation gorge on mountain ash berries while they listen for ravens feeding on gut piles. Bald eagles ride the wind over Nasukoin Mountain and thread their way eastward through the continent's spine to winter on the Missouri, Saskatchewan and Yellowstone. November's full moon marks the peak of the mule deer rut. And when wind-sheared larch needles glow golden on the snow Bull and Cutthroat trout are running back down to Flathead Lake after spawning in the headwaters. In the same way that these creatures and events are interconnected, this ecosystem is seamlessly interwoven with every other ecosystem on earth.

Although young hunters are typically bloodthirsty, most of us grow out of it as we learn to see and appreciate the connections in the natural world. Teddy Roosevelt and Aldo Leopold, who were ardent killers in their youth, matured into visionary conservationists and ecologists. But the ethical traditions and tenets of land use that these men and their peers endorsed have been overwhelmed by consumerism. Culturally, we applaud environmental protection as long as it doesn't hinder the economy or infringe on our "rights". We talk about the need to live within the limits of the land but insist that we "own" it. The supposedly benign recreational use of natural resources has become as oppressive and industrial as good old-fashioned mining or logging. Hunters aren't immune from this affliction. Advertisements in sporting magazines promote machinery and gadgets that will help us bag a "monster bull" in the "hotspots" described in the articles. Animals are increasingly seen as commodities, valued chiefly for the size of their antlers. And in the most deplorable example of this attitude, some so-called "hunters" pay exorbitant fees to shoot captive trophy animals.

As game management has become more politicized, hunters are preoccupied with defending hunting seasons, and have lost sight of the need to conserve habitat and wildlife. But quality hunting opportunities will disappear if we aren't more concerned with what is left on the land than what is taken from it. And the spirit of fair chase will disappear if we can't voluntarily constrain our use of technology. The dilution of a conservation ethic among hunters is a subtle but potent threat to hunting's future and may be irreversible in light of current demographic trends.

Just as the hunting community's empathy with nature has been jaded by consumerism, many resource managers, through no fault of their own, aren't the woodsmen that our ancestors were. Many college graduates in forestry or wildlife management don't know how to log, trap, fish or hunt. Their educations focus more on the abstract than the practical, and many of their professors aren't connected to the land.

Observant outdoorsmen and–women could help resource agencies tailor scientific knowledge to site-specific situations by providing pertinent information gleaned from familiarity with a place. The Montana-based Orion Institute advocated this approach in a 1999 newsletter: the organization is "developing monitoring concepts that will utilize hunters for reliable documentation of key wildlife species. No other group covers remote terrain more regularly, extensively and systematically than do skilled hunters."

Although the "ologists" and bureaucrats have been conditioned to favor scientific data and to dismiss anecdotal observations, they are beginning to acknowledge the value of indigenous knowledge and the political need to seek public input. They are also charged with the thankless work of protecting resources during a time of rampant consumerism. Hunters should encourage resource managers to favor conservation over exploitation. We should be their allies rather than their adversaries.

An old man once told me something which complements Robert Ruark's quote in the preface to this essay. After listening patiently while I griped about going to school, and threatened to quit, he said, "No you stay at it. After all, knowledge is a light thing to carry." As a lifelong hunter, I appreciate the wisdom in his words. The experiences and insights we bring into camp after each day's hunt are also easy to carry. Like snowflakes, they are individually delicate but collectively powerful, imperceptibly accumulating into knowledge which can help us fill meatpoles, freezers and pantries, and provide sustenance for body and soul, family and friends.

Ultimately, our success as hunters can be gauged by the vitality of a conservation ethic within the hunting community. This ethic has to be grounded in an intimacy with the land, an appreciation for its beauty and a reverence for its inhabitants. Without this sensibility we are merely consumers, blinded to our kinship with the Earth, willing to sacrifice it at the altar of the economy. But if we embrace, rejuvenate and pass on the ethics which engendered the hunting opportunities we enjoy today, we can consider ourselves successful, by any standard of measurement.

"Bugle" magazine, July–August 2001

Saw Shop Dharma

I BOUGHT A COUPLE OF NEW HUSQVARNA chainsaws a couple of weeks ago, along with an extra bar for the smaller saw. As it happened the bar didn't fit, so I went back to the shop to exchange it. A mechanic I wasn't familiar with got the correct bar, and installed it, and the chain, on the saw. When he was adjusting the chain he showed me how much slack to leave in it, and told me I'd have to readjust it as the chain stretched with use. He was imperious, and condescending. It rubbed me the wrong way, so I cut him off before he was finished, and said "You know I've cut timber for over forty years, so I think I've got this figured out." There was another mechanic behind the counter who knew me. He laughed and said, "Yeah I spose you do." I sensed by the way he said it that this wasn't the first time his co-worker had rankled a customer. The guy who was working on the saw shoved it across the bench to me, slid his wrench into his pocket and walked away.

I was on a slow burn when I got into the pickup, but on the drive to work I realized how I had let my ego mishandle the situation. I thought, maybe I should have patiently listened to him, and thanked him for his advice. But doing this with a sarcastic attitude would also have been ego-driven and insulting, whether he knew it or not. Or I could have just kept my mouth shut. But if I had been offended by being mistaken for a greenhorn my silence wouldn't have been respectful.

The best thing I could have done was to accept his help, even though he had an odd way of offering it and give him my heartfelt thanks. After all, he had a lot to teach me.

March 2019

Fading Trails

SOME DREAMS ARE CREATED from fragments of daily experiences; they can be instructive or meaningless, funny or terrifying. Others are undiluted by trivia and come from a dimension that's inaccessible to our conscious mind; they may give us insights that change our lives. I've been blessed with many of these dreams. They've arrived when I needed them most. I learn from them, and I'm compelled to walk through the doors they open. In some of them, especially those concerned with hunting, the boundaries between humans and animals are blurred; we shape-shift back and forth into one another. This archetypal perception is illustrated in pictographs and primitive sculptures, showing humans with wings and the heads of birds, or animals with human faces. For me, the message of these dreams is that a universal energy, or spirit, flows through and between everything that exists, and that this spiritual connection is especially strong between hunters and our prey.

The most memorable of these dreams came to me about twenty years ago, in an elk hunting camp in the Big Hole. In this dream I was hunting elk in open sagebrush hills. I was on a trail traversing a steep slope. I heard something move below me and stopped. A cow elk climbed the hill, stood in the trail, and turned to face me. I lifted my rifle, centered the scope's crosshairs between her eyes, and flipped off the safety. As my finger crept toward the trigger, the elk changed into an adolescent woman, about the age of my daughter. Her eyes were dark, like an elk's, and her hair was black. Her buckskin dress was tawny yellow, the color of elk in November.

I dropped the rifle, appalled at what I'd nearly done, but relieved that I hadn't pulled the trigger. I knelt in the trail, sobbing uncontrollably. The young woman came to me and hugged me. Then many generations of Elk People appeared, seeming to rise from the earth. As they encircled me I was given to understand that hunting, killing and eating them was my role in a rite of communion that united us through flesh, blood and spirit. The dream was vivid, visceral, unforgettable. I hunted the next few days, but my heart wasn't in it; the imagery of the dream had rattled me, and it kept haunting me. Over the course of the winter I wrote an essay about the dream, entitled "Communion," and sent it to "Bugle" magazine, the publication of the Rocky Mountain Elk Foundation. In it, I recounted the dream, and concluded with these paragraphs:

"Looking through the veil of this dream, I see elk as husbands, wives, sons and grandmothers. Reliving some hunting experiences, I watch death cloud a mother's eye while I kneel beside her in the blood-soaked earth. I cut the heart of someone's daughter out of its translucent sheath and hang it up to cool, slipping the aorta over a spruce limb. I hear the last breath of a grandfather trail off into the morning breeze.

"The dream is terrifying and inspiring; but most of all it is humbling. I see that life cannot be taken unless it is first given. I know that this exchange is sacred. And I wonder if we can ever be thankful enough."

"Bugle" bought the essay, and I went on with my life. The dream was always on the edge of my mind, but I chose to focus on the sense of kinship I had felt with the Elk People rather than the episode with the girl. It was nearly two years before "Communion" was published, because the editor was apprehensive about how it would be received. He referred to this in a companion piece to the essay:

"But the last thing we want is to turn readers away from this magazine, and more importantly, from the Elk Foundation. The conservation challenges before us are too big. We need every elk hunter who cares. And there's no shortage of hunters who care about protecting elk country but want nothing to do with articles which try to, as Bob Love puts it, 'confront the paradox of killing animals we love.'"

The editor's intuitions were valid; most of his readers disparaged the piece. A few were so offended by it that they cancelled their subscriptions, along with their memberships in the Elk Foundation. The reaction among my friends and acquaintances was the same; a man who I assumed would be receptive to the message of the dream spoke for most hunters

I know when he said, "You need a different dream." But my friend Michael said, "Every hunter should have that dream." Like me, he saw it as a gift.

I wasn't surprised by the response to the essay. Our culture disregards the significance and power of dreams. It also assumes that only humans have souls, or spirits; so anything that isn't human—animals, trees, water, soil—is a commodity that we can exploit without fear of spiritual retribution. Hunters who grow up believing this way are merely consumers, obsessed with what they can kill with as little effort as possible. The only difference between them and the market hunters of the nineteenth century is that many modern hunters are more concerned with trophies than meat.

Conservation-minded hunters are less visible and vocal, and more introverted than our counterparts. Although we're outnumbered, we're determined to protect wild country, and to preserve the skills, ethics and traditions of our hunting heritage. This is necessary and timely work, but it will be fruitless if we don't reconnect with the spiritual aspects of this heritage.

The spiritual connections we share with the animals we hunt is genetic, passed down from thousands of generations of hunters who preceded us; our Cro-Magnon ancestors honored these relationships, and kept them alive, in their art. The relentless industrialization of nature has frayed and severed these connections to such an extent that we're in danger of becoming aliens on our own planet.

We should all be thankful that the spiritual affinity between animals and humans is being nurtured, like an ember in a dying fire, by a few people living in the remnants of hunting cultures that still exist. Several years ago, on a beautiful October morning, I was taking part in a sweat lodge ceremony with some of my Blackfeet friends. Before we began, the leader asked if anyone wished to speak. My friend Ira said, "Yes, it's hunting season, and I'd like us to pray for the spirits of the animals who are killed and treated without the proper respect. We need to seek their forgiveness, so they'll come back and offer themselves to us again." Ira wasn't judging thoughtless hunters--to him they were like children who didn't know any better--he was worried that their behavior would generate negative spiritual energy, making it harder for everyone to provide for their families.

Hunters are conduits between animals and humans; through us, in an ancient ceremony, one life flows into many others. We have to kill cleanly, care for the meat properly, and use as much of it as possible. If more hunters can learn to perform this part of the ceremony it will be a step in the right direction. But the ceremony isn't complete until we celebrate our spiritual kinship with the animal; we have to apologize before we kill it, thank it afterwards, make offerings to its spirit, and handle the remains respectfully. The fact that most hunters will dismiss this suggestion as mysticism shows how far our society has strayed from the ethics and customs of authentic hunting cultures.

The trails to the spirit world are fading fast. Hunters have to walk them again and keep them open so the animals can return and offer themselves to us. Those of us who believe that we should receive the gift of another being's life in a sacred way shouldn't be discouraged, even though we're seen as crackpots. Our dreams will teach us the ceremonies and give us the courage to follow our hearts.

Grandpa's Gun

GRANDPA PAID $18 FOR THE WINCHESTER Model 94 .30-.30 in 1926 and hunted whitetails with it in southwestern Pennsylvania until he died in 1954, before I was a year old. It was hung on some barn nails driven into the red oak rafters of Grandma's attic, along with his squirrel gun—a Remington Sportmaster .22—and a Nitro Express double barrel 12 gauge that he used for rabbits and grouse. My brother Tom and I were fascinated with the guns, and spent a lot of time studying them, even if we weren't allowed to handle them without supervision. They were a tangible connection to our Grandpa, who we knew only through stories and photographs. Grandpa had carved seven notches in the forearm of the Winchester. Neither Dad nor our uncles knew what the notches meant; Grandpa killed a deer nearly every year he hunted with the rifle, so they thought maybe the notches signified bigger bucks.

Grandpa killed a buck with the rifle the first year he hunted with it, and had the head mounted on a walnut board, above an oval mirror. The buck's feet were arranged in a line below the mirror, bent at right angles to serve as coat hooks, with some brass hat hooks below them. The buck didn't have a huge rack, but it was oddly shaped; one antler was normal while the other was flat, and slightly palmated, like the deer had slept on it when the antler was in velvet. The mount hung on the wall in Grandma's house, by the front door, at the bottom of an oak staircase. Every time Tom and I scrambled down the stairs, we'd jump up when we hit the last one, and touch the buck's nose. Eventually the brittle skin cracked, exposing the plaster filling. Grandma wasn't fond of the mount, especially when its nose started peeling, and always threatened to put it in the cellar. She often told me, "If you like that deer so much you can have it when you grow up." My parents stored the mount in their basement when Grandma moved out of her house, and I brought it to Montana when I eventually settled down. It hangs on the wall of our front room now, its nose refurbished with some wood glue and shoe polish. Besides the mount, I have some photographs of Grandpa with his rifle and the buck; one was taken in the woods, and the other was taken in town, with the buck draped on the front fender of a Model T.

I hunted with the Winchester in Pennsylvania, but never killed a deer with it. I brought it west with me when I finished high school and shot a mule deer with it in the mountains near Bozeman. The following summer my Uncle Frank gave me his .270, a Model 70 Featherweight outfitted with a Bausch and Lomb 2.5-8 scope, that he'd bought in the mid-50s. He said, "This will work better than that .30-.30 in the country you're hunting now." When I brought it home and told Dad that Frank had given it to me, he said, "He must have rocks in his head." When I took it to George Dieruf, a cranky old gunsmith in Bozeman, and asked him to help me develop some handloads for it, he said "That's an awful nice gun for a Damn Kid." Uncle Frank was right; it was the ideal rifle for western hunting. Dad and George were also right; it was an outrageous gift for a kid. But even though I was too naive at the time to really appreciate the Model 70, I knew enough to take care of it. I've hunted with it now for forty years and have killed more game with it than Frank could have imagined, in places he would have loved to hunt.

I didn't use Grandpa's gun much once I got the Model 70, especially when I started hunting mountain mule deer. These muleys tend to hang in the timber, but they live in big country which can offer some long shots. With the scoped .270 I could both make the long shots and thread a bullet through a doghair lodgepole thicket if I had to; it is simply a more efficient tool than the .30-.30. This was an important consideration when I was raising a family and didn't have a lot of time to hunt. But now that the kids are grown, filling the freezer isn't as critical as it once was, and I use the .30-.30 more often. Killing a buck at two hundred yards with the .270 is no problem, but it's more like sniping than hunting. With the .30-.30, I have to stalk the deer, or rattle them in, preferably within 75 yards.

The Model 94 is sleek and well-balanced; a pleasure to carry in the woods, even if it is a little heavy. The stock, with its curved steel buttplate, is too short for my build, but I'm reluctant to alter it. I rigged a Butler sling on the gun though, making it more practical for mountain hunting. Although it's eighty-five years old, the .30-.30 still shoots well, especially with my handloaded 170 grain Nosler Partitions. Grandpa used to sight in on a brake drum hung from a tree limb, figuring that the drum is about the same size as the target area of a deer's chest. I use the same method, shooting offhand at various ranges. My aging eyes can't draw a very fine bead with the buckhorn sights anymore, but I can hit the steel consistently. Pinpoint accuracy isn't as critical as getting within range and having the patience to wait for a good shot.

One Thanksgiving morning several years ago I decided to take Grandpa's rifle for a walk in the mountains. The Thanksgiving hunt is a tradition I was raised with and maintain to this day. In Pennsylvania we hunted small game on Thanksgiving, as deer season hadn't opened yet. Tom and I bird-dogged for Dad and our uncles before we were old enough to carry guns, then hunted with them when we came of age. It was a good excuse to get out of the house while the women were preparing the feast; fifty years later, it still is. In Montana, the general big game season ends on the Sunday after Thanksgiving. The bucks are in full rut, and if we've had heavy snows the muleys are bunched up on their winter ranges. On this particular Thanksgiving morning my son, Orion, went with me. He'd killed a buck earlier in the season, so he was acting as a spotter, rattler, and, hopefully, a dragger. As we drove up the road towards our muley hunting territory, Orion said "If you get one I'll drag it out for you. I owe you for all those bucks you drug out for me." I wasn't going to argue with him; the first buck he killed was a rangey four-point, and by the time I got it to the road, after wrestling it off the mountain through windfalls and vine maple thickets, it seemed as big as a Shetland pony. He killed a couple more like that before he'd grown enough to get them out on his own, and I often wondered why he couldn't give me a spike or a forkhorn to work with occasionally.

We parked the pickup, and started hiking up the mountain, through the alder slides and into the timber. The faint trails we followed were only game trails, but they were familiar; I'd started hunting here thirty years ago, when Orion was a baby.

Now he and his sister Keeley are grown, and both of them are healthy and strong, thanks in part to the meat this place has provided over the years.

As Orion and I climbed, we stopped frequently to catch our breath and cool down.

Orion lightened my load by carrying the binoculars and rattling horns. He glassed and rattled each time we stopped. The ground was mostly bare, making for quiet walking. The wind was in our favor, blowing mostly downslope, sometimes tinged with the scent of deer. Eventually we got into more snow, latticed with muley tracks and trails. We stopped on a ledge that offered a good view of the country. The sun had climbed enough to highlight the ridgeline above a draw to our west, dispelling the shadows from the timber on the sidehill and in the bottom. A black cloudbank on the horizon signaled an approaching storm, but for the time being the sky was clear, so the deer would be up and feeding before they bedded down in sheltered thickets. Orion rattled a little, and we watched the draw. We were just about to head out when he spotted some movement, which materialized into a four-point buck, who walked out into a clearing in the spruce bottom about 200 yards away. He was headed uphill, tilting his head like he was preparing to spar with another buck, even though he was the only deer we could see. Orion rattled once more. The buck stopped and looked in our direction. He wasn't interested enough to come to us, but he wasn't spooked, either; he just slipped into the timber and vanished. He had spotted us, so it would be futile to chase him; we might see him, but not at close range. Orion was kind of put out and said, "We could have had him easy if you'd brought your big gun". I was thinking the same thing; that was a good buck, and the sight of him had my adrenalin going. But I said, "Then we'd be finished hunting. If we keep climbing we'll find more deer, and maybe even see him again."

We kept walking up the narrow ridge, stopping frequently to rattle. At one point, when we were scrambling up through some ledges below a bench, we heard a buck snort and take off downwind. We could still hear him crashing through the lodgepoles when we made it onto the bench, and saw from the tracks that we had probably rattled him in. The buck had come downhill to investigate but blew out of there when we got too close. We weren't more than twenty yards from him, but never saw him, thanks to the terrain.

As we climbed, we approached a broad basin at the head of the draw. The country was more open, with bunchgrass parks and scattered Doug firs. It was the perfect place to find deer late in the morning, feeding before a storm. We stopped on a bench, shrugged out of our packs, and had a snack. We chewed on some jerky I'd made from a buck I'd killed up here a year ago.

The weather was raw, but we were comfortable, hunkered in the lee of some large firs. Orion rattled for about twenty minutes, to no avail. We decided to head out. As I stepped out from the fir grove I saw a buck coming up out of the draw towards us, not running, but moving fast, like he was looking for a fight. When I stepped behind a tree to get into shooting position the buck spotted me and stopped about 75 yards away. I leaned up against the fir and cocked the hammer on the .30-.30. The buck was facing me, with some brush obscuring his brisket, and only his upper neck exposed. I was hoping for a closer, broadside, shot, but the buck was suspicious; weaving his head around, trying to catch our scent. I sensed he was going to bolt, so I took the shot he offered me. The shot felt good, but the buck didn't go down. He lurched down the hill into a fir thicket and staggered up out of the draw below us, about 40 yards away. Again, he only offered me a neck shot, but at least he was broadside. I followed the buck with the gun, and when he stopped, I shot him behind the ear. The crack of the .30-.30 was muted by the wind, but we could hear sticks cracking and scree clattering as he slid down the draw. While I levered the shells out of the magazine, Orion said "That old gun really packs a punch!" We followed the skid trail down the draw and found the buck piled up under a fir windfall. We broke some limbs that he was hung up on, and he slid down to a flat spot where we could dress him out. We found that the first shot was off by a couple of inches, and had just grazed his neck, but the second shot was instantly fatal. Although the buck was in rut, he was still fat, and I guessed he would dress out about 230 pounds. His rack was dark and heavy; a standard four point for this place, with about a 24-inch spread. Orion built a fire while I worked on the deer. By the time I was finished the fire was cranking. We sat by it, eating lunch. Some gray jays flew in and started picking at belly fat. We were in no rush to leave; it was better to be out here than to be underfoot in the house on Thanksgiving.

We knew the draw below us was laced with windfalls, so we cut off the buck's head, and his legs at the joints, to help him slide better. I offered to pack the head, but Orion insisted on making good on his promise, and lashed it to his day pack. I sauntered down the mountain with Grandpa's gun, enjoying the scenery, while Orion thrashed through the windfalls above me. The buck's heart rested in my pack, warm and heavy against my back, but my own heart was light. The meat these mountains had provided would sustain us in the coming year, until next Thanksgiving, when I hoped to be here again, chewing on some of it I'd dried into jerky.

The next day, as I cleaned and oiled the .30-.30, I thought how using Grandpa's gun was like going hunting with him. Although he'd never hunted anywhere but the Appalachians, the gun was imbued with his spirit. In that sense he was with me, hunting muleys in the northern Rockies. Orion pulled in just as I was slipping the .30-.30 into its case. He asked if he could take it on a late-season elk hunt near the Sun River. I gave it to him, along with twenty rounds of ammunition, and he went off to get his camp gear together. Orion saw some elk on that hunt; he couldn't get within .30-.30 range, but he had fun trying. And I bet his great grandpa had fun helping him.

Edited version published in **'MT Outdoors'** *Sept/Oct. 2012*

Orion, The Deer, And the Dream Time

WHEN I WENT OUT TO CHECK the weather that morning I knew this was the day we'd been waiting for; there was something in the air, a familiar voice telling me that the hunting would be good. Silhouetted by faint starlight, the clouds that had been jammed up against the Divide for a week were beginning to break up and head east. We could expect one clear day, maybe two, before the next front blew in from the coast. The mule deer rut was at its peak, so the bucks would be roaming, searching for receptive does. With the change in the weather the mule deer would be drifting towards the winter ranges, following trails their ancestors had carved into the mountainsides; the herd moving like one being, guided by an ancient, inborn intelligence that linked each animal with the other, and the present with the past. Everything felt right.

My son, Orion, had turned twelve the past February, and this was his first hunting season. He woke easily and dressed while I cooked breakfast. It seemed like I'd been preparing for this day his whole life. Before he could walk, I'd carry him into the woods to connect him with the earth. When he was older, we'd wander through the doghair lodgepole flats behind our house. Sometimes we'd stop, and I'd ask him to point to the river, the bridge or the house. I was teaching him to keep his bearings subconsciously, to nurture and trust his intuition, despite what his rational mind told him so I didn't have to worry about him getting lost. By the time he was in grade school he was able to navigate pretty well on his own. Once when he was out back with Inez and some of her friends, he led them back to the house, despite their insistence that he was going the wrong way.

Our family's lifestyle is shaped by the wild country around us. Orion and his sister Keeley were strong hikers, avid anglers and deft berry pickers by the time they were in grade school. And most importantly, they were comfortable being outdoors. I bought Orion a single shot .22 when he was eight, and he learned the basics of gun safety and shooting. He'd bought a used Model 70 .270 in March with earnings from his wood-splitting business and we spent many summer evenings reloading and shooting. He had confidence in the gun and his ability, and I knew he could hit game if he got close enough and waited for a clear shot.

It's not difficult to teach someone how to shoot, and kill, but you have to work on a deeper level to teach them how to hunt; how to take another creature's life with the necessary reverence and respect. it's a learning that comes from time spent outdoors, watching and listening, just being there, observing the connections that create the web of life. It's a state of mind, and a place of mind.

To the Australian aborigines, this place is the Dream Time, when totemic beings imbued creation with their spirits, and transformed a barren, featureless landscape into the Earth. Stories about these ancestors, and ceremonies honoring them, preserve the culture's connections to the land and transfer knowledge that is essential to survival in a climate where agriculture is impossible. Although technology has numbed our senses and distracted us, some of us still hunt, fish and gather wild food. We know when the whitefish run, where the huckleberries ripen first, and where you can find them later in the season, when the elk are bugling. We know that whitetail fawns are born when the first wild strawberries appear. We listen when red squirrels and ravens talk to each other and try to learn their language.

When you're hunting properly you enter the Dream Time. You're acting more from your heart than your mind, with no ego cluttering things up. The Inuit hunter waiting motionless for hours at a seal breathing hole, a cougar stalking an elk, and a coyote, listening with his head cocked, to a vole travelling under the snow are hunting in the Dream Time. For a skilled hunter, the real challenge of hunting isn't finding his prey, but finding the Dream Time. He enjoys being there far more than he enjoys killing. The hunter's prey nourishes his body, but the Dream Time nourishes his soul.

Orion and I spent the early part of hunting season in the Salish Mountains west of home; short trips in gentle terrain that strengthened his legs and got him accustomed to packing his rifle in the woods. I killed a whitetail buck on one of these trips, which allowed me to spend more time guiding him. We started hunting muleys in the Whitefish range in mid-season. The weather was mild, so the deer were scattered and hanging high. The hunting was fruitless, but pleasant. And it was time well spent; Orion was learning the country, getting stronger, and tuning into the rhythms of the mountains.

Driving along the North Fork River that morning, I noticed that the snow level on the peaks hadn't dropped for a week. We'd have to climb fairly high before we found deer, but I was confident that Orion could make it if we took our time. Dawn was breaking when we left the pickup and headed uphill. We had to travel through some alder slides and yewbrush thickets before we got into the bunchgrass parks and open Doug fir where the muleys hang out. Even with me breaking trail, the snow was crotch-deep on Orion.

We rested when we broke a sweat, trying to keep our scent down. Devil's club stalks marked springs that we could hear flowing under the snow, and chickadees pecked at alder catkins in the morning shadows. The deer would be feeding too, not far from their beds. After an hour or so, we had made it through the worst of the brush and came to some shale ledges that were the steepest part of the climb. We threaded our way up through them, following deer trails, and took a breather in a grove of wind-bent firs when we crested them. I saw something move about 100 yards above us, and with the glasses made out the hind leg of a doe. She was feeding in a maple thicket with a few other deer. They winded us, and headed uphill and west, but weren't terribly spooked.

The morning breeze was blowing from the east, and rising from the drainage below us, so it was futile to follow the deer. To have any chance of getting close to them we'd have to head east, while climbing above them, then when the wind shifted with the approaching front, we could hunt into it. Once we were above them, with the wind in our favor, we could get the drop on them. The sun wasn't quite overhead when we reached a sidehill trail which would put us above most of the deer on the mountainside. The wind was howling in a gray sky, and the temperature was dropping. We hadn't seen any deer, or much sign of them, and we were tired and hungry. I sensed the barriers of the "real world" dissolving. I was entering familiar territory, but it was brand new to Orion. We were slipping into the Dream Time, becoming invisible.

We took a break and ate some trail mix in the shelter of some stunted Subalpine firs. The wind tapered off, and for a few minutes we could hear the stream roaring in the canyon below us. The wind picked up again, but it was blowing from the west. This is what we'd been waiting for, and it came at the perfect time. I smelled deer in that wind: the raunchy urine of rutting bucks and the musky scent of does in heat. I tasted shredded willow bark ground into antler. I saw the wind lifting the hair on their backs, and the glint of winter sunlight in their black eyes.

I told Orion to chamber a shell and go ahead of me. We sidehilled along for a few hundred yards, stopping every few steps, slipping in and out of the timber shadows. A fat spike buck walked out on a ledge fifty yards uphill and stared at us. I'm sure he'd never seen a human. He was standing behind a fir windfall, with only his head and neck visible.

We waited for him to move so Orion could get a clear chest shot. Then a 4-point with bone-white antlers and a narrow, high, rack emerged from a serviceberry thicket and stood beside the spike. Orion still couldn't get the shot he wanted through the tangle of brush and limbs. The 4-point winded us and took off with the spike on his heels. We stayed still and let things settle down, hoping they hadn't alarmed any deer that might be ahead of us.

We continued down the trail and came into a small park fringed by large Doug firs. The spike was eating grass by a broken-off snag, but his friend was making tracks; I caught a glimpse of him as he dove into a doghair thicket in a draw ahead of us. Orion lay down to get a steady rest on a windfall and aimed at the spike, who spotted us and walked behind the snag. I whispered to Orion that it was his decision whether to shoot or not, that the deer would offer himself if it was meant to be. Orion said he couldn't kill the spike because he seemed like a child. We watched him and waited, sensing that we were surrounded by deer. The storm was building; frost-burnt balsam root leaves rattled and rasped in the wind, beard lichens hanging from the fir limbs waved like river grass in a restless current.

A doe stepped out of the timber about fifty yards away and walked into the park, with a massive 4-point buck walking stiff-legged behind her. He was like a mythical being, swollen-necked and red-eyed. Power radiated from his dark, heavy antlers. They seemed to be alive. He felt our eyes on him, spotted us and stopped. The dream deepened, and we looked into each other's souls.

Orion flicked off his rifle's safety. The metallic sound was harsh and foreign in this world of wood, bone, rock and antler. The buck walked towards the doe with his neck stretched out. After two steps, he paused. Orion squeezed the trigger and hit the buck in the heart. The bullet rocked him, but he didn't drop; he was dead on his feet, but too strong to die. Orion shot him once more, in the neck. The buck piled up and slid past us in the snow, his antlers clattering on rocks, flopping and crashing through the timber until he slid into a windfall 100 yards downhill. The silence was sudden, and profound.

I slapped and pounded Orion on the back and he yelled, "I got a deeeer!", drawing the word out like he did when he was learning to talk. I'd killed plenty of game but had never felt the magic so intensely; I was ecstatic, awestruck, speechless. We slid down to the buck and thanked him for giving himself to us. We stroked him and hugged him and watched his eyes turn blue and glassy in the winter wind. We knelt in his blood and worshipped his power.

Camprobbers and chickadees drifted in from the trees and talked with us while we cleaned the buck. We fed them chunks of fat, our frozen fingers tingling from the heat of his blood. And when we were finished we headed down the mountain, the buck tobogganing through the snow, the broad trail blood-flecked, scented with fresh-turned earth and crushed fir needles.

Along the way we stopped on a ledge to rest. Orion touched the buck and said, "He's in Heaven now." And I saw that in this place, at this time, we were all in Heaven: that the blood in the snow and the blood that stained our knives and hands was our blood, and the water that boiled from the springs and roared through the rocks in the gorge and held the sky in the beaver ponds was also our blood, and the blood of these mountains, and the wind that blew streamers of snow off the cornices on the cliffs was our breath, and the breath of these mountains, and of the deer. And I saw that as long as fathers pass this knowing down to their children and show them how to make their living from the land with gratitude and humility, the world will be right, and one life will fold into another until the end of time.

Dream Canoe

SEVERAL YEARS AGO I dreamed that my friend Bruce and I were paddling a canoe up a semi-frozen river. The river was deep and narrow, with strong currents. Broken ice chafed and hissed under the canoe. Snowbanks marked the water's edge along each shore. At one point the river turned to our left, with the main current piling up against a sheer wall of ice to our right. As we muscled our way through whirlpools on the inside of the bend I saw a moose skeleton, which appeared to be made of crystal, embedded in the ice wall. Each bone was distinct and in place and glowed with an inner radiance. I wanted to touch it, and spend some time with it, but I knew we would drown in the attempt. We weren't making any headway as it was, and just when I thought the current would overpower us, the canoe twisted somehow, so we were underwater, upside down, but still paddling upstream. We surfaced in a shallow bay of a large lake. It seemed to be evening, but it was hard to tell what time of day it was, like it is when sunlight absorbs wildfire smoke, and feels heavy.

There was no breeze, and no sound other than water dripping from the blades of our paddles. The lake reflected the dull ocher light of the sky. There was a point of land in the distance across the bay, and we paddled towards it. As we approached, people came down to the shore to meet us; parents, toddlers, elders and teenagers. They were native people, clothed in smoked buckskin. They welcomed us with smiles and laughter, as if we were old friends.

Several of their wolfish dogs circled me, wagging their tails and rubbing against my legs; one of them stood on his hind legs, rested his front legs on my shoulders, and licked my face. Somehow Bruce and I got separated, and I wound up with a group of people who wanted to show me something. We walked through the village and followed a trail that led through an old burn, where aspen, birch and willow saplings grew under an open blue sky. Then we entered an older spruce forest. It was cool and dark. Ferns and moss lined the trail. Eventually we came to a small clearing, where there were four white pine trees, huge and ancient, so tall that their tops faded into the sky. They stood in a circle, illuminated by the same radiant light as the moose skeleton. I was overwhelmed and honored to be in this sacred place. Then I noticed that the people and dogs had vanished. And when I looked back up at the trees, I saw that they were dying before my eyes; the lush blue-green needles shriveled to reddish brown, drifted through the bare limbs and rained down on me. The supple black bark turned gray and flaked off the trunks. The fragrant resin dried into beads, and cracks, like the ones that lightning makes, spiraled up the trees. Then I understood that everything here was dead. This dream was like others I've had, where I canoe across a lake to the Other Side, but they weren't as powerful and memorable as this one.

The dream visited me one morning last summer in northern Saskatchewan. I was canoeing with Bruce and two other friends, Steve and Jim. Over the years we've taken several trips in the region south of Wollaston Lake and north of the Churchill River. Our route this time was a loop which began and ended at Otter Rapids on the Churchill River, in the country northwest of Missinipe.

We paddled upriver for a day, then turned north, traveling west, and then south, through a series of lakes and small rivers. After a week or so we were back on the Churchill, two days travel upstream of where we'd left it. We met a group of canoeists at Trout Rock portage who had been running the rapids there, a quarter mile stretch of standing waves averaging about eight feet tall. They were on the river to run whitewater and were paddling Royalex canoes with spray skirts and flotation. But we weren't paddling whitewater canoes, and the river was running about two feet higher than normal, with more current. We'd have to portage around several sets of rapids, and if we weren't careful the high water could sweep us right past the take out points.

We camped at Trout Rock that day and continued downriver in the morning. The water was fast, but not dangerous. We made good time and set up camp in mid-afternoon. After supper we looked at the map and talked about the next day's journey. There were portages marked around three sets of rapids, but the map didn't show portages around several others. These would be considered navigable under normal conditions, but it might be risky for us to run them in high water.

The next morning I woke up before daylight and started the breakfast fire. Then I went off to a quiet place by the river to sit with my pipe. My friend Dan had given me the pipe at the Sun Dance in June. It was the fifth year we'd danced together. He said, "A friend of mine made this pipe for you. Whoever smokes it will have their prayers answered." Initially, I didn't pack it with my gear because I didn't want to risk breaking it or losing it. But it was beginning to speak to me, and I was learning to listen. So when the pipe told me to carry it on the trip, I did. I smoked it every morning at dawn and at sunset every evening. I invited the spirits of the land to smoke with me and share their prayers.

While I was sitting there that morning I watched how the smoke floated over the river like a blanket. It would hang there for a moment before it was carried away by a subtle breeze that rose from the flowing water. The river was breathing in the prayers that came through the pipe. I thought of the time some of us Sun Dancers were soaking in the Two Medicine River after the ceremony. Dan said "There's no such thing as new water. It's all ancient, and it's all been prayed over. Every river carries prayers." I pictured the prayers travelling down the Churchill, and into Hudson Bay. I pictured them swirling through whirlpools, plunging into the holes below falls, rising as mist above the foaming whitewater. I heard them in the faint roar of the rapids downriver. Then I was in the dream, and it was in me: I was paddling up the river. Broken ice hissed along the hull of the canoe. The moose skeleton was just out of reach. The canoe turned upside down, and I was in that bay, in a lake of another world. I didn't cross the bay and didn't want to. I could see the village, but there was no sign of life. Then I returned to the Churchill, where I was sitting with the pipe. I knew that the dream had come through the pipe, from the spirits of that place, and that it was a warning: we had to be cautious and mindful in the coming day, especially when we were opting to run rapids or portage around them.

The dream shadowed me while we broke camp. When we got on the water it was more tenacious—I was on the Churchill one moment, on the dream river the next. I was wary, but not afraid. We portaged twice before mid-morning on trails that were marked on the map. A few miles downstream we came to a set of rapids that looked manageable, but we couldn't see the whole stretch. We landed on a point on the south shore, walked downstream, and saw that the lower end was too rough to run. There was no portage trail on that side. The north side of the river was slower and calmer. We considered running that side, but the whirlpools at the tail end of the rapids, where the river swirled into a deep hole, concerned me, and I said so. We could probably make it, but what if we didn't? If we swamped we might get stuck in an eddy and drown. And if we were able to swim to shore, we'd likely be stranded without food, gear or canoes; hapless pilgrims waiting to be rescued—a humiliating penalty for using poor judgement.

My friends thought I was being too cautious, but they agreed to consider portaging. We studied the map and saw that if we crossed the river and portaged northeast across a point of land we could bypass these rapids, as well as another set that began around a bend in the river. While we talked, a young black bear came out of the alderbrush on the other shore. He strolled along the bank for about twenty yards until he came to a grassy spot, then waded into the river and drank. To me, he was telling us to portage, and showing us where to land. When the bear wandered off we paddled to the grassy spot. Jim and Steve stayed with the canoes in case the bear decided to raid our food packs. Bruce and I scouted for trails; I walked along a sidehill above the river and Bruce stayed close to the bank. After walking about a half-mile I heard some rapids below. I dropped off the ridge and found a good portage trail. Walking back upriver I met up with Bruce and told him that the trail started at the other side of a small bay off the main river. He'd found a route to carry around the upper rapids, get back on the river and follow a side channel into the bay. By midday we'd completed both portages. We ate lunch in the shade of some jack pines, where a bear, maybe the one we'd seen, had been excavating ant nests. The air was scented with crushed blueberries and shredded pine roots. There were no more rapids to run that day, and there were portages around the rapids further downriver. I was relieved that we hadn't had any mishaps. The dream was still with me, but it was no longer ominous. Looking at the river seething through the gorge below our lunch spot, it occurred to me that the dream was channeling my thoughts in the same way that the ancient bedrock of the Canadian Shield channeled the currents of the Churchill.

In this area the Churchill is more a series of lakes than a conventional river, but when you're paddling across these lakes you see whirlpools rising to the surface and feel currents shifting the canoe. You're still on the river but floating above it. Eventually we entered the western end of Nipew Lake. The lake was as flat as a mirror. The heat was oppressive, even though the sun was blurred by wispy cirrus clouds. I napped while I paddled. Lulled by the surge and glide of the canoe, and the rhythm of water dripping from our paddle blades, I was in the dream, crossing the bay. By midafternoon we were in the main part of the lake. We landed on a rock island about a quarter-mile offshore to stretch our legs. There was one tree on the island—a windswept, gnarly birch—with a lush carpet of kinnikinnick growing beneath it. We sprawled out in the shade and slept for an hour or so, then set off.

A few paddlestrokes brought us to the eastern point of the island, where the slabrock met the water. I noticed a white bone lying on the gray rock. Then I saw the entire skeleton of a cow moose, with most of the bones intact, from skull to tail. It must have died in the spring and been picked clean by eagles and ravens. If it had died in the winter wolves traveling on the ice would have scattered the bones. The skeleton made the dream more tangible. It was an affirmation, a signal that the spirits were trying to get my attention. But why? Maybe I'd lived here in a previous lifetime, which might explain why I had an affinity for this country, why some lakes and campsites seemed familiar and pleasant to me, while other places had an air of malevolence and darkness about them. Was my spirit reconnecting with friends and family in the dream? Was the skeleton their way of welcoming me home?

I was pondering these questions as we continued down Nipew Lake. At one point when we were paddling side by side, Bruce mentioned that Alexander McKenzie traveled up the Churchill in 1789 on his way to Great Slave Lake, and that somewhere near here he'd passed by a village littered with bones, where all the people had died of smallpox. So he named this place Dead Lake.

My mind tried to process the implications of this information, but it could only tell me that we were on Nipew Lake, on an afternoon in mid-August. We'd followed a map to travel here in our Kevlar canoes. But we might not have made it without the help of the spirits who came in the dream and shared the pipe that morning. There's no map to the Nipew Lake where those spirits live. You have to ride there in a Dream Canoe. Only your heart knows the way.

September 2017

Aurora

I

KAH HAD BEEN HUNTING for one turn of the moon, roaming in circles, further and further outward. But the moose had vanished; he could not catch their scent, or cut their trails, or find their beds.

Sometimes he snared a squirrel or a hare, but there was little strength in their meat, and he was tiring. At the end of each day, boneweary and disheartened, he made fire beneath a spruce and ate what meat he had, chewing it with frozen cranberries. Leaning back against the flame-warmed bark he would drift into sleep, and wake, shivering, in the glow of the coals. When he built up the fire the smoke braided its way skyward through the spruce boughs, where the aurora shimmered behind the stars, like minnows swimming in the sun across warm sand shallows. He watched them turn into animals he knew: wolverine, lynx, wolf and black bear; marten, otter, beaver and muskrat; moose, caribou, kingfisher, eagle and weasel; lake trout, char, pike, and whitefish. Moonlight passed through them, flowing over the snow like the blood of spirits. He sang his medicine songs to the moose and called them in, but when he shot at them with his bow the arrows couldn't cut them.

One night he saw the future in a dream. He watched wolves cracking his bones with their marrow-stained teeth, blue flies boiling in his eyesockets, and chickadees weaving his hair into their nests.

Each morning Kah rose and walked into the wind, beginning another circle, and each night, having wandered deeper into unknown territory, he stared into the fire, wondering why his luck had left him. His senses were sharp and his mind was clear. His arrows were straight and well-fletched, their flint heads flaked to cut clean. And his bow was strung with the finest sinew. But he couldn't find any moose tracks, or where they had nipped the redwillow buds, or where they had broken the river ice to sip the softroaring water.

As he traveled there were fewer signs of life: no alders gnawed by hares, or spruce cones shucked by squirrels, no jays visiting with one another. The creaking of his snowshoes hung in his trail like scent, betraying his presence, and when the frozen birch branches clattered in the north wind, warning of a storm, he felt like the only living creature in the world.

II

One morning a raven flew in low circles over his camp, speaking to him. Kah watched and listened, and answered him, doing the best he could to speak Raven. When the raven knew that Kah understood him, he lifted from the spruce and flew. Kah followed him. Every so often the raven stopped and talked so he could track him. They traveled this way in the forest through the day, until they came to some muskeg, where there were alder thickets and scattered larches. The raven was waiting for Kah in a spruce snag and flew off as he approached. When the raven was nearly out of sight, at the far side of the swamp, he swooped, then rose, and circled back to the snag. He looked down at Kah and spoke softly, his voice like water running under deep snow. Kah knew what he was saying. He strung his bow, drew an arrow from his quiver and checked the wind. It was faint, and in his favor. He walked towards the spot the raven had marked, staying in the shadow of the forest. The moose was feeding when he saw her, facing away from him. He nocked the arrow and stalked her, close enough that he could taste her scent.

Sensing Kah's presence, the cow turned broadside and looked at him, her hooves squeaking in the snow. Lifting her head, she snorted through her nostrils. Kah drew his bow. The frost in the bowstring cracked under the tension of the flexed birch. The raven watched from the snag, murmuring. Kah released the arrow. It sank feather-deep into the cow's chest. She wheeled, and ran, disappearing into the alder brush. The raven lifted from his perch and flew after her. Kah waited, giving the cow a chance to lie down and bleed out. In the distance the raven was talking, but Kah could only hear snatches of his voice, like he was chanting. When the light began to fade Kah followed the cow's trail. Beads of blood were sprinkled along the left side, where she was wounded, and further along he saw where she had coughed up a froth of bright lung blood. He found her lying on her side, pawing at the air with her front legs. The raven was perched in a larch. He cocked his head and looked at Kah. Putting his hand to his heart, Kah thanked him, and they watched the cow die. Her last breath caught in a gurgle of blood, and her legs stopped moving. She didn't blink when Kah touched her eye with the tip of his bow. He pulled the arrow from her chest and sucked blood from the wound as her pulse ebbed and stopped. It felt like the sun in his belly.

Kah slit the cow open and dragged out her entrails. He ate slices of her liver and heart.

The raven picked fat from her stomach and kidneys. Night fell, and Kah crawled into the steaming cave of the carcass, the scent of blood sweet and heavy in his nose. Cradled by the cow's ribs, with his head at the base of her windpipe and his feet tucked into her pelvis, Kah slept. In the larch, the raven kept watch as dry snow fell, rasping through the frozen alders, covering every trace of their passing.

III

That night the aurora flowed through the stars like colored wisps of smoke. Inside the carcass, Kah couldn't see them, but he dreamed them. They wove themselves into an Eagle whose feathers shimmered like rainbows, whose eyes were like fire behind blue ice. The Eagle swooped, snatching Kah in its talons. Kah watched the earth shrink beneath him as the stars blurred past in swaths of light. They came to a place where the stars faded into the dawn of another world. There was a birch tree at the center of that world. Its canopy supported the sky. At the top of the tree a branch grew in each direction. Four branches, spanning the horizons. Four rivers flowed from its roots: red water in the eastern, yellow in the southern, green in the western, blue in the northern.

The Eagle dropped Kah in the place where the tree branched. He circled the tree, screaming; the only sound in that world.

Swirling wind rose in the wake of his wings; the only wind in that world. Kah looked up through the birch leaves fluttering in the wind, and saw pieces of sky, bluer than any on earth. Then he saw the Eagle descending on him, still screaming, wings and talons flared. The Eagle pierced Kah's chest with his talons, pinning him to the tree. He plunged his beak under Kah's ribcage and tore out his heart and lungs, sliced his belly open and ripped out stomach, liver and intestines, plucked Kah's tongue from his throat, drew his brain out from his eyesockets, then stripped the flesh from each bone.

Kah watched this from a place outside his body. He saw the pieces of his body falling like rain into the rivers, and his blood flowing down the tree, into each river at its source. And then he was traveling in the rivers, each part of him feeling as one. The water carried him.

He was sipped by deer, moose, elk and caribou, and lapped into the red throats of wolves, foxes and bears.

He was drawn through the feathered gills of trout, tasting their cold moss-scented blood.

He was sucked into the roots of plants, emerging from the darkness of the earth into leaves that greened the sunlight, flowers that scented the breeze, berries that ripened in the summer sun.

He flew over mountains in wind-driven clouds and returned to the earth, falling through rainbows.

He was dew, beaded on a spiderweb at dawn.

He was frost, splitting granite.

And he was fog, rising in the breath of streams.

He was the spray on the crest of a whitecap, the foam in the curl of a breaker.

He rested in lakes and traveled in rivers.

He was frozen in blue glaciers and drawn by the moon through the oceans.

He was blood and milk, rain and snow, sap and nectar, sweat and tears.

The water carried him.

And each piece of him died, and was reborn,
until he knew the lives of all things,
and saw how they all shared the same Spirit.

IV

One day Kah's pieces came together into a salmon,
swimming upstream to her birthplace. She was resting in a pool
when the Eagle's shadow darkened the streamstones. As the
talons pierced her skin, threaded through her ribs and clasped
her spine, Kah remembered who he was. The Eagle soared, and
the salmon's last breath became a lone cloud in the empty sky.
Rain fell from the cloud, and sunlight passed through it, brilliant
with the hues of the aurora.

V

Kah opened his eyes. The cow's skeleton clasped him like a
pair of hands. Wisps of sinew hung from the ribs, fluttering in
the morning breeze. He smelled thawed soil, melting snow,
swollen alder buds, sun-warm larch bark. Kah crawled out and
stood, wobbly like a new-born fawn His arms and legs tingled
as the blood surged through them. Chickadees flitted back and
forth, carrying tufts of moose hair to their nests. Gray jays
pecked dry fat from the backbone,

The raven called from the spruce snag. Kah answered him.
The raven appeared and perched on the ribcage. Cocking his
head, he listened while Kah told him about the Eagle, and the
Tree, and his journeys in the rivers. When he was finished, the
raven lifted from the bones and flew.

Kah gathered his knife, bow, and arrows, and followed the
raven. And as he walked, everything he saw called him Brother.

A Few Words for Our Friend Bud Moore

VICKI ASKED ME TO SPEAK about Bud's spiritual side, because as she put it, Bud and I were spiritual brothers. We shared many of the same interests, but the most important thing we shared was an affinity for what Bud called the "spirit of the land." Spirits are ingrained in the land. In wild country they're more apparent, and easily sensed. In a developed place they still exist: we just have to be more receptive to connect with them. Take this place, for instance: Before there was a city and this building, grass and wildflowers grew here. The seasons turned, free of clocks and calendars: glacier lilies bloomed at the edge of melting snowdrifts, balsamroot flowered about the time mule deer fawns were born, chokecherries ripened when the sky hazed with wildfire smoke, whitefish spawned when the larch turned gold. Imagine what happened here: A band of elk grazed on some fescue and bedded down. Old ladies dug camas bulbs. Kids passed through on their way to the river to catch cutthroats. Coyote pups played in the sun. A grizzly bear dug ground squirrels. Someone was born here. Someone died. Moments like these, blending and aging over time, form the spirit of the land. One life folding into another, endlessly. Our flesh is soil, our blood water, our bones stardust. We are connected. Related. We belong. We don't disappear when we die, we just change into new clothes. Bud didn't "go" anywhere. We just have to think differently to see him. Let's honor this place, and this gathering, and our friend, with a moment of silence.

I discovered Bud sometime in the late 1960s, when I was a teenager. I was at home in western Pennsylvania, reading an issue of National Wildlife. There was an article in it by Bud, and a photo of him approaching a muley buck he'd just killed. I remember thinking "I'm going to meet this guy someday." Well, unlikely as that might have seemed, it did happen, and when it did the timing was perfect. After spending twenty years working as a timber faller, I was uneasy, and often heartsick about what I was doing to the land. As a cog in the machine of industrial forestry, I was manipulated by bureaucrats, mistreated by corporations and demonized by environmentalists. I knew there was a way to get logs out of the woods and leave a functioning forest behind, but I also realized that proving this point would be an uphill battle, in light of the fact that the timber economy is geared towards extraction rather than stewardship. But since my situation was intolerable, I either had to set off on my own or find a new career. This is when Bud entered my life. He inspired me to leave the blazed trail and follow my heart into new territory. And he confirmed my intuition that working in harmony with the spirit of the land was the surest path to security and happiness.

Modern culture doesn't honor the life force of the land. This is why we are becoming aliens on our planet. Our attitude seems to be darkened by an aura of pessimism. Bud recognized this collective sense of despair, and agreed that it was often warranted, but chose to channel his energy in a positive direction. He encouraged us to restore our ties to the land. He knew that becoming native to the earth again was not only possible, but imperative. He was excited that this awareness was growing in our culture.

Tom Parker and I had an experience about fifteen years ago that confirmed Bud's optimism. We were attending the Seventh American Forest Congress in Washington DC. This was a four-day event aimed at discussing and resolving forestry issues. There were hundreds of people there, from all over the country. At a panel discussion about National Forest management, a Sierra Club dignitary told the audience that policy decisions were best left to the professionals; that local input was irrelevant. The audience seemed to agree with him, but that didn't stop Tom and I, with Bud at our sides in spirit, from raising a ruckus. We probably didn't change any minds, but at least we livened things up. As we were leaving the room after the presentation a woman pulled us aside. She was a member of the Hoopa tribe, from northern California. She said "When I was a little girl my grandmother told me a prophecy; how one day there will be people living among us who aren't Indians, but understand how we think, and will care for the land like we did. She called them Earth People. Listening to you guys, I can see her words coming true, and it makes me glad." Bud was an

Earth Person. He dedicated his life to creating a world of Earth People, and he did a good job of it.

In "A Sand County Almanac," Aldo Leopold wrote, "I have read many definitions of what is a conservationist, and written not a few myself, but I suspect that the best one is written not with a pen, but with an axe. It is a matter of what a man thinks about while chopping, or while deciding what to chop. A conservationist is one who is humbly aware that with each stroke he is writing his signature on the face of his land. Signatures of course differ, whether written with axe or pen, and this is as it should be." Bud was skilled with both pen and axe, which was a rare talent. But his tolerance, his appreciation of diversity, further distinguished him. Bud didn't judge people or try to change them. He did something more difficult, and more powerful. He taught by example.

I'll get out of the way now and let Bud speak for himself. Here are the last three paragraphs of The Lochsa Story:

"Not many have touched the Lochsa and escaped the land's great spirit of place, and realization is growing that nature's ways have to be respected if we are to prosper very long. The quest for understanding nature can never end, for humans will never fully solve the mystery of it all. Everything in this land, including ourselves, is so intricately connected to everything else. The important thing is that while we continue to harvest the land's bounty, as we must, we keep on learning as we go.

We must take time now to deepen our understanding of the consequences of what we have done and are doing to the land. Within our reach lies untapped knowledge whose exploration, together with lessons drawn from the successes and failures of the past, offers us a remarkable opportunity to draw closer to the earth. By doing so, we of the Lochsa—and people everywhere for that matter—can continue to live and prosper in harmony with the land.

Three young ground squirrels chased each other among the boulders. The clouds darkened. I saw a glint of lightning behind the crest of the Grave Mountains, far to the south. The land oozed life, and its fresh breath rippled the surface of the lake. I suppressed an urge to hike out along the ridge and beyond, into the depths of a new frontier. To do that takes more than one lifetime. A raindrop fell. I looked around at that great expanse, feeling the natural power that had shaped so much of what I am and what many others are. Then I lay down in the beargrass and listened to the wind."

December 2010
Missoula, Montana

Ceremony

OUR FRIEND KERRIE had been in ill health for the last two years, thanks to the lingering effects of radiation therapy she'd received as a teenager. She was in her mid-fifties and had been forced to retire from her career as an elementary teacher. Although the radiation cured her Hodgkin's Lymphoma, it had compromised her immune system, creating a condition where fluid built up in her lungs and around her heart. Kerrie's doctors prescribed steroids to alleviate the inflammation, but ultimately, there was nothing else they could do. Despite using oxygen, it became more difficult for her to breathe. About six months before she died, Kerrie's health began deteriorating more rapidly, and it became increasingly apparent that the end was near.

We've known Kerrie and her husband Steve for nearly twenty years. They were married at our place on Thanksgiving. At their request, I performed the ceremony, with our friends as witnesses. I wasn't really surprised when Kerrie asked me if she could be buried on our place. She'd grown up in a dysfunctional family and had many fears. Our family and home offered her stability and security. Beyond that, Kerrie was a free spirit, who distrusted and resisted many conventional social practices. Regarding her own funeral and burial, she was determined to be in charge, to avoid the funeral industry as we know it. She wanted a homemade funeral.

Inez and I talked it over, and consented, provided the procedure was legal, and that we could do it without interfering with any plans our children might have on our seven acre tract. After some thought, I settled on a place not far from where Steve and Kerry had been married. It was near the western boundary of our property, and not likely to be disturbed in the future. Beneath two large lodgepoles there was an open area of pine grass ringed by some younger trees—spruce, Doug fir and White pine.

Kerrie had been fretting about her funeral and burial and wanted to see the gravesite once I'd located it. Steve brought her out on a Saturday afternoon in mid-September. We drove as close as we could but had to walk about eighty yards through the woods. Kerrie was weak, so we took our time and visited along the way. When we arrived at the grave site, she was wobbly. She looked around and said, "You won't have to cut any trees will you?" I said "No, I can work around them, and we'll plant some grass and wildflowers once we've filled the hole in." She said, "It's a good place," then asked, "But how will you dig it if the ground is frozen, or if there's a lot of snow?" I said, "Don't worry. I'll figure it out." Kerrie didn't say anything else; she just looked at me. I sensed she was handing me something. I hoped I would be worthy of her trust.

A few days later Steve asked me if I could make some kind of litter to transport Kerrie to the grave. She didn't want a casket, and suggested that we stuff her body into a sack she stored her yoga mat in. But since we had to carry her some distance, this would have been an awkward arrangement. I fashioned a litter with Lodgepole saplings that I cut on our property. I peeled them, then lashed them together. It was rustic, but serviceable, and met with her approval.

In the following weeks I visited Kerrie several times. She was cautious about seeing people because of her weakened immunity, but she never seemed worried about me. Earlier in the autumn I'd given her two eagle breast feathers that had been given to me by a friend who had prayed and fasted with them during the Sun Dance. I'd fasted with the feathers as well, and kept them hanging in a window in my cabin. Every so often I'd smudge them with sage and sweetgrass and pray with them. I thought the feathers might help Kerrie stay strong and keep her thoughts clear as she prepared for her journey. I explained all this when I gave her the feathers and showed her how I smudged them. At first she didn't understand that they were hers to keep. She thought I would want them back when she died. She cried when I said, "No they're yours now." Whenever I visited she asked me to smudge them. She kept them in a soft buckskin pouch that was always nearby, usually hanging around her neck. She would give me the pouch, and I would take it outside, and smudge the feathers. The feathers connected us.

In the second week of October I sensed that I should dig the grave. I considered doing it with hand tools, but this wasn't practical, because the scant topsoil in our neighborhood is underlain with hard packed sand and gravel. I made arrangements to rent a mini-excavator. The machine was delivered on a Friday afternoon and I planned to use it on Sunday. I had to replace a starter on a machine on Saturday morning. What should have been a simple job became more involved, and I wound up chasing parts. I was near Kerrie's place at one point so I stopped in. Inez was there. There was something different about Kerrie which I couldn't put my finger on. Her eyes were darker, more liquid. But she was lucid, and happy, laughing and joking with Inez. She asked me to smudge the feathers. When I brought them back in I handed them to her, and hugged her goodbye. There was no warmth in her skin, and her bones felt brittle. I looked back at Kerrie when I opened the door to leave; her body was transparent. Shimmering. Like a dragonfly's wing.

I dug the grave the next morning, Sunday. I made it seven feet deep; as far as the excavator would reach.

The packed gravel made for tough digging, but at least it didn't slough, and I was able to make a neat rectangular hole. I piled the dirt away from the sides so we could carry the litter over the grave and lower Kerrie in. I managed to work around the young trees and didn't have to cut any of them. When I was finished I realized I had to cover the hole; we could get a sudden snow storm or an animal might fall in. So I bridged it with some two by fours and laid three sheets of steel roofing across them.

I hosed the dirt off the excavator, parked it and went in for some lunch. Inez called from Steve and Kerrie's. Kerrie was slipping in and out of consciousness, but this had happened a couple of times recently and she had always rallied. I did some chores around the place that afternoon, but my mind was on Kerrie. Inez called about six and suggested I come over. Kerrie seemed to be in a coma.

The house was full of people when I arrived. Some I knew, some I didn't. They were taking turns going to Kerrie's bedside, touching and speaking to her, though she wasn't responsive.

When I had a chance I went to her. I could see a wispy shadow around her; Kerrie's spirit, clinging to her body. Kerrie was there, but she wasn't. She was in two places. The pouch with the feathers was tucked in beside her. I took it outside and smudged the feathers in my usual place, a large block of purple argillite under a willow. The moon was rising from a red cloud in Bad Rock Canyon. The sage smoke was blue in the starlight. I put the feathers back in the pouch. Steve came out and asked me what I thought. I said, "This is it." He said, "But this has happened before, and she's always come out of it." I said, "Not this time." I hugged him and we cried together. I smelled fallen cottonwood leaves on the night air. I pictured Kerrie as a dry leaf clinging to a branch, at the mercy of a grain of frost, or the slightest breeze.

Steve and I went back into the house. Everyone was gone except Inez and Meg. I went over to the bed and pulled the blankets back. Kerrie's hands were folded across her chest. I tucked the pouch back in beside her, crushed some sage to bring out the scent and put it in her hands. I covered her up again and said, "It's o.k., you can go now." It seemed like she could hear me, and wanted to respond, but couldn't. Her breathing was regular, but thin and shallow.

Steve said he and Meg would be fine, so Inez and I went home. Steve called around six with the news that Kerrie had died at three-thirty. While we fixed breakfast Inez told me about a dream she'd had about Kerrie right before Steve called; she looked healthy and said "I don't know why I was so worried about dying. There was nothing to it, and I feel fine." I wasn't surprised; I knew one of us would dream about her.

Steve wanted to bury Kerrie that afternoon, around four. Although we'd made some preparations, there was a sudden sense of immediacy we hadn't experienced until now. Kerrie was actually gone. She had to be prepared for burial. Steve had to get a death certificate, and deal with the authorities. Someone had to notify folks and organize a potluck. I had to create and prepare for a ceremony. We were all improvising.

Steve made some phone calls and was directed to the sheriff, who said that since Hospice had been involved, there was no need to call a coroner. Meg went to Kalispell and got the necessary documents.

Inez met our friends Gail and Mary over at Steve's. They washed Kerrie, and anointed her with oil, even though none of them were experienced with the procedure. Inez said they "just figured it out." They dressed her in clothes Steve selected and covered her with a shroud Mary had sewn. Steve stayed with Kerrie until Michael and Stevia arrived to help him bring her out to our place.

I drove over to the place I was working and cut a pickup load of Grand fir boughs so we could line the bottom of the grave with them. When I got home I removed the cover from the grave and threw in several armfuls of boughs. Then I slid an extension ladder into the hole and climbed down. The fragrance of the boughs was overwhelming, intensified by the damp stony air. I worked carefully, and quickly, not quite trusting the gravel. I thought "If these walls cave there'll be two of us in here." When I had spread the boughs evenly I looked up. Compressed into a narrow slot by the grave edge, the sky was abnormally blue, nearly dark enough to see stars. Some gravel clattered down onto the boughs when I climbed up the ladder, but the walls held. Looking down into the hole, I realized we would need some rope to lower the litter. We'd also have to tie Kerrie to the litter so she wouldn't slide off in the process of getting her to the grave and down into it. I found two hanks of three-eighths manila in the stack of hunting camp gear and took it down to the grave. I dropped one end in and figured how much slack we'd need. With the two hanks of rope I cut four pieces for lowering the litter and had another left for tying. It was almost as if the rope had been custom made for the job. I'd found it on a trail a few years ago and always thought it might come in handy; who would have guessed I'd be using it to bury a friend? I looked for a sign from Kerrie all morning, but nothing caught my eye. The sky was empty of eagles. No coyotes appeared. The ravens were just being ravens, clowning around while I worked.

Once the grave was ready, I did some pruning and leveling in the clearing where Steve and Kerrie had been married so we could set up tables and chairs and build a fire. While I was gathering firewood I heard my friend loading the excavator on his trailer. I'd considered backfilling the grave with the machine, but it seemed more sensible, and more in line with Kerrie's thinking, to do it by hand. I wasn't sure when or how that would happen but trusted it would work out somehow. Inez drove down with chairs and tables and I helped her carry them over to the clearing. Then I went up to the house, wolfed down an apple, showered and changed into clean clothes. Steve drove in just as I was lacing my boots. We went into my cabin. I smudged the feathers one last time. Then we just stood there, silent, in the sage smoke. It was like we were awake in a dream. I heard cars pulling in, voices outside. I said, "I guess we've got to do this." Steve put the feathers back in the pouch and we went out.

Kerrie was lying on the litter under the canopy in Steve's pickup. We considered driving her down but opted to carry her. We slid the litter out of the pickup. Michael and Stevia held their end while I tied Kerrie to it. Her eyes were open and she was smiling; like she was about to make a wisecrack about getting the rope too tight. The darkness I had seen around here last night was gone, displaced by a subtle radiance. She seemed healthier and happier than she had for some time. Her death was suddenly immediate, and real to me, but I couldn't let that interfere with the task at hand. Michael, Steve, Stevia and I hoisted the litter. I heard women crying. Someone came over and placed a wild rose branch on the litter. The rose hips were lustrous, as brilliant as rubies, perfectly complementing the colors of the shroud.

We carried the litter down the road towards the grave. Crossing the creek, I heard water trickling through the latticed twigs of the beaver dam. The pond was skimmed with yellow willow leaves. I pictured how some of us in this procession had walked here before, in another procession, on Steve and Kerrie's wedding day. We made our way to the grave, following a faint trail that had appeared during the course of preparing the site. We put the litter down when we got to the edge of the grave. I tied the lowering ropes to the four corners of the litter using bowline knots and checked to make sure they were tight. I smudged Kerrie with sweetgrass, then sage, and put the smoldering sage at the head of the grave, the west end. Then we each took a rope and lowered the litter, careful not to tip it, until it rested on the boughs, and let the ropes fall in.

I knelt beside the grave. Everyone was standing, expecting me to say something. I didn't have the strength to stand, or speak, or look at anyone. But kneeling in the fresh dirt, in the fragrant sage smoke, grounded me, and helped me find some words. I looked down at Kerrie and just said what I was feeling: that last night Kerrie was in two places. Now she was in the spirit world, which is like another room, right beside us, that we seldom see. She really didn't "go" anywhere. We could see her if we learned to look and think in a different way.

Steve spoke next. He thanked everyone for their help and prayers. He talked about Kerrie. Somehow he maintained his composure. He took the feathers from the pouch, explained their significance, and dropped them into the grave. They fluttered down and came to rest beside Kerrie's right arm. I invited other people to speak. When everyone had finished I said, "Now we should cover her with these boughs. Anyone who wants to help, can."

I had a big pile of boughs at the foot of the grave. A few people came forward, and then everyone joined in. The energy that had been building among us as we all stood there in grief and shock was like a looming thunderhead, but the work of covering Kerrie with the boughs had cleansed and focused it. The aura of our gathering was brighter, and healthier. Inez stepped forward with a wooden bowl full of flower petals from Kerrie's Garden and ours. She talked about Kerrie's love of gardening, scattering some of them onto the boughs. The bowl was passed around, so everyone could bless Kerrie with petals. A few more people spoke, then it was time to fill in the hole.

I had three or four shovels and a couple of Pulaskis leaning against a tree. Those of us with tools had an impatient audience waiting to spell us. Stevia and I went up to the shop and found more shovels, as well as a rake, a pick and a couple of hoes. Stevia said buckets might work, too. The tools were snatched up when we got back to the grave. There was barely room for everyone to work. Those without tools formed a bucket brigade. People began pacing themselves. The energy was less frantic and more deliberate; conversations emerged, then there was laughter. Before we knew it the grave was filled and raked smooth. In the process, the young trees had been protected, and the dirt had been raked from around the beargrass and kinnikinnick that had been covered during the excavation.

The women had set up a kitchen near the fire. It was hard to believe so much food had appeared on such short notice; the tables were laden with soups, chili, bread, pies, cake, coffee, beer and wine. We ate and talked around the fire, and people started drifting off towards sunset. Just before dark I walked over to the grave. There was a raven feather in the trail; a perfect tail feather. I thought "Well it's about time. I've been waiting all day for you to leave me a sign." I picked up the feather and slid the quill into the loose soil at the head of the grave.

Inez and Steve and I went up to the house and visited until midnight. Before we went to bed we walked down to say good night to Kerrie. In the moonlight, the raven feather had the sheen of obsidian. Four wolves howled, and kept howling. Kerrie was on her way.

Journal Of a Feral Shaman

I WAS RAISED in western Pennsylvania near the town of Beaver, where the Beaver River meets the Ohio, about thirty miles downstream from Pittsburgh. At that time, during the fifties and sixties, the steel mills were running full tilt. But the economy was thriving at the expense of the land. Although the air was cleaner than it had been in the early part of the century, it was still hazed. The Ohio and Beaver rivers and many of their tributaries were fouled by sewage and industrial effluent. The headwaters of these tributaries were somewhat healthier, and were populated by salamanders, crayfish and minnows, but even the most remote creeks were tainted by chemical fallout, as were the forests, fields and soils. I couldn't prove this but knew it intuitively. Growing up, I was plagued by allergies and ear infections. When I left the area, even for a short time, these problems disappeared, and I had more energy and a better attitude.

Despite all this, I was attached to the place. My dad worked in the city but was a naturalist at heart. When I was midway through the first grade he built a house a few miles out of town. It was a good place to grow up; there was a narrow band of civilization along the township road, but between there and Route 51, about two miles to the north, there wasn't much besides woods and a few working farms. This swath of undeveloped land continued west about fifteen miles to the Ohio state line. To my brother and I, this was a virtual wilderness, and our dad encouraged us to get out in it; we fished, rode horses, built forts, dams and treehouses, and hunted snakes, salamanders, frogs and crayfish.

Thanks to my dad, I got interested in conservation. This was in the mid-sixties, when writers like Sig Olson and Aldo Leopold were influencing natural resource management. When I joined Boy Scouts I got to help in actual conservation projects; we made brush piles for small game, cut browse for whitetails and did stream restoration work. Through the merit badge program I learned the fundamentals of ecology, and became aware of the connections between animals, people and the environment. My formal education seemed bland in comparison to camping and working in the woods, but I had a sixth-grade teacher who made school enjoyable for a little while. He was an authority on local history, especially the frontier period.

We spent some time studying the Native people of the area. We learned how their cultures had thrived here for thousands of years, and how they had been affected by European settlers.

Given this historical perspective, I looked at the industrialized landscape around me and imagined free-flowing, clear rivers you could drink from; clear sky and air you could breathe. Walking through the scraggly woods and bramble thickets encroaching on abandoned fields, I pictured ancient forests of oak, beech and maple. We had wildlife in the woods: cottontails, squirrels, ruffed grouse, pheasants, a few whitetails, foxes, groundhogs, coons and possums, but at one time there'd also been bears, wolves, bison and elk. I lived in Beaver County, near the Beaver River, but actual beavers were nearly extinct. Driving to Pittsburgh we'd pass through Baden, where the railroad switchyard was built on the Indian settlement of Logstown. And there had been another Indian town at Aliquippa, where the J&L Steel complex sprawled along the Ohio for six miles. The two primary roads in our township, Tuscarawas and Dutch Ridge, followed Indian trails. Walking the trails in the hollows, I sensed the spirits of hunters and war parties. I also sensed the spirits of the earth. Outside is where I felt most at home.

Visiting this parallel universe and getting out in the woods with the Scouts helped me cope with the distractions of adolescence (hormones and girls) and comply with the civic standards that were imposed on me (school and church). We went to the United Presbyterian church, out of allegiance to my mother's Scottish heritage. Dad went along to get along, so church attendance was compulsory, and we seldom missed a Sunday. It wasn't until I joined Scouts, and would be off camping somewhere for the weekend, that I was granted amnesty. This wasn't a blanket amnesty though—the Scout troop was sponsored by the church, and the adult leaders felt obliged to perform a service when we were in camp. But compared to the real deal, this was anarchy. The service was typically brief, and generic, and I was outside; unwashed, squinting in campfire smoke, wiping my nose on my shirtsleeve with impunity.

Besides being monotonous, the conventional church services were forgettable. The minister and I were both to blame for this; he was boring, and my mind was usually elsewhere. In spite of my daydreaming, the basics of Judeo-Christian religion, as interpreted by the United Presbyterians, seeped into my consciousness, where I retained a few highlights: the gory battles of the Old Testament, the barbarism of the Crucifixion, and some of Jesus's parables. During a Palm Sunday service, when I was eleven or twelve, I was studying a palm frond and half-listening to the story about Jesus riding through town on a donkey. I imagined the scene—the palm trees growing in the oasis, the houses made of mud, the sand and the sun—and asked myself "Why does any of this matter to me? It happened a long time ago in a desert somewhere." I don't know where the question came from, but it caught my attention. The morning light was streaming through a stained-glass window near our pew. There were some small vent windows above the sill that were open, and I could feel the breeze flowing through them. I smelled greening grass and snow-rotted maple leaves. I heard a robin, and a barking dog. There were some silver maples growing in the narrow yard between the church and the street, their bare branches silhouetted behind the stained glass. I was taking all this in when another question came to me: "What was the religion of the people who lived here before us?"

I think this was the first time I wondered if there were any religions other than "ours," meaning Methodists, Baptists, normal (not United) Presbyterians and Catholics. I didn't know any Catholics, since all their kids went to parochial school. But I knew something about them, as Grandma Alexander had told me that Protestant and Catholic kids would form gangs and fight each other when she was a girl in Scotland. I learned about Jews in Sunday school and church, but didn't know any, and assumed they all lived in the desert with the Egyptians, Greeks and Babylonians. My grasp of religion and geography may have been flimsy, but I knew that the religion I was being indoctrinated in had been imported from a foreign culture and landscape. This made me suspicious, and reluctant to buy much of it. I didn't need a minister or a church to teach me about God. To me, the autumn colors in the Appalachians were more inspirational than any stained-glass window. Tadpoles wriggling in a scummy pond were more miraculous, and interesting, than the Genesis story. The skinned bear carcass hanging in front of Bus Weimer's Gulf station in Rockwood had the crucifixion beat hands down. And how could a fish created from thin air, even with a loaf of bread on the side, compare with an iridescent bluegill caught with a Zebco? To me, the beauty and magic of nature was miraculous: especially so, because it was tangible. Reading about Indian cultures, I discovered parallels between their spiritual beliefs and my intuitions. But the Indians were long gone from our area. Like the beavers, the names of some of the towns and rivers were the only remnants of their existence.

As a teenager I felt increasingly alienated from the culture I was immersed in: a culture obsessed with materialism, arrogant and ignorant, determined to overpower, not honor, nature. I couldn't change any of this, but I didn't have to like it. I was fortunate to have woods to roam in, and to have a father and uncles who taught me how to hunt and fish and love the land. Thanks to Boy Scouts, I learned how to live and travel in the woods, and I got to see country that was wild in comparison to Beaver County. As far as school went, I was an indolent student. Learning how to tie knots, start one-match fires, sharpen axes and paddle canoes seemed more practical than chemistry or calculus. Biology wasn't so bad but I never learned how to tell a red oak from a black oak in the classroom. I was an avid reader, though. My father subscribed to Outdoor Life and Fur Fish and Game, and had a fair sampling of camping, woodcraft and natural history books in his library. My horizons broadened when he subscribed to National Wildlife. Like most beginning hunters and fishermen I was bloodthirsty. The hook and bullet publications catered to this mindset, but National Wildlife, with a more ecological focus, led me into new territory, where I discovered "A Sand County Almanac" and "Walden." These books, more than any others, reflected my spiritual beliefs. It was heartening to know that I wasn't alone, or insane. In my junior year of high school I took a comparative religion class, taught by a lapsed Jesuit priest. Part of the attraction of this course was that the teacher was widely considered to be a subversive character. He introduced me to Buddhism, meditation, Alan Watts and Lao Tzu. Buddhism seemed more sensible than Christianity, but it wasn't earthy enough to suit me. It wasn't rooted in the soil I knew.

After high school I headed to Montana with a friend. Our idea was to study wildlife management at MSU. He eventually got a degree, but I washed out in three months, and switched my major to creative writing. Montana was clean and wild compared to the Beaver Valley. I moved into a ramshackle house out of town which had no insulation, plumbing or electricity, and lived off the land as much as I could. I built a sweat lodge next to the house, more for practical reasons than anything else, as it was an effective way to get clean. I came to appreciate the spiritual realm of the sweat, but with no heritage, or teacher, I could only go so far. I started working as a timber faller, living in a tipi in the woods near the job sites. The best thing about my time in college was that I met Inez and convinced her to marry me. We moved north to the Flathead valley, where she was from. I continued working as a logger, we bought some land, built a house and raised two children. We've been married for thirty-five years now. Our son Orion is thirty-one, our daughter Keeley is twenty-nine. Inez has worked as a teacher for twenty-five years and I've been in the woods for thirty-five. I spent twenty years working for industrial logging operations and was often uneasy and heartsick about what I was doing to the land. In the mid-90s I went off on my own, determined to practice sustainable forestry. It hasn't been easy, but I feel better about my work, and have managed to provide for my family.

The decision to break from the traditional logging community wasn't easy. I was working for a good friend who paid me well, and I had a family to support. But I wasn't satisfied with my job; sometimes we did some worthwhile work, but usually we were paid to annihilate the forest rather than care for it. This was draining me physically, mentally and spiritually.

I had a dream that made the decision for me; a dream that was as memorable and powerful as the experience I had in the church on Palm Sunday. In the dream I was standing on a mesa in a desert landscape. It was nearly dark, and the sky was a dull maroon color. In the distance I saw a shimmering blue wing. It came over to the mesa and hovered at the cliff edge. There were some people standing behind me. I turned and said, "Do you see this?" They said, "No, there's nothing there." I said, "I'll show you," and I went to step out on the wing, but just before I did, I looked down. It was thousands of feet to the ground. I was terrified, and hesitated for a moment, but then I took the step, and there I was, standing on the wing. I woke up immediately, knowing that everything would work out if I followed what my heart knew was right.

Not long after the dream I was working on my dozer in the yard and my friend Larry stopped by. We'd cut timber together at one time but, I hadn't talked with him for several years. He said, "I don't really know why I stopped. Something told me to I guess." We visited about the usual stuff for a while, then he asked me "You ever heard of an Indian sweat lodge?" I said "Yeah, I've built some and done it on my own, but I've never done the real thing." Larry said he'd been sweating with some folks on the Blackfeet Reservation and told me a little bit about the ceremony. He said he'd call sometime if I wanted to go, and we said goodbye. He happened to look up just before he opened the door to his pickup, and said, "Someone's listening." I looked up, and saw a bald eagle circling, no more than a hundred feet above us. We watched the eagle until it drifted off towards the river. We talked some more. Larry said he wasn't comfortable talking to most people about his sweat lodge experiences, but, "For some reason, I felt like I could talk to you about it, and that I should talk to you about it."

That was nearly fifteen years ago. I've been honored and blessed to take part in the sweat lodge and other ceremonies. The people I sweat with are like family to me. Some are Indians, and some aren't; it doesn't matter as long as you're respectful and your intentions are good. My friends have encouraged me to learn their ways, not so I can become an Indian, but so I can be a better person. Prayer is a big part of their tradition, and everyone is encouraged to do this in their own way. The way I see it, the universe and everything in it is imbued with a life force, or spirit: "God is a verb" is how Buckminster Fuller phrased it. My idea of prayer isn't so much asking for this or that, but being open to this universal spirit, so it can flow through me and I can direct it where it's needed. There's a spot near my cabin where I go in the morning. After I smudge with sweetgrass, I turn sun-wise, stopping at each of the four directions. I think of people I know in each direction, my children, my relations, my friends. I picture the land, the rivers, oceans and animals. I just try to send good thoughts out. All I ask for is the strength to accept whatever happens without judging. When I complete the circle I do the same with the earth, and the sky. This is how I ground myself and prepare for the day. If I'm faced with a big challenge or if I'm asked to pray for someone, I go to a certain place on a mountain. It's not easy to climb up there, but it's a powerful place. Some of my friends are healers, who follow what they call the "Pipe Way." They use their pipes to pray or fast for people, to send healing spirits to them. I don't claim to have any healing power, but if someone asks me to pray for them I do my best, in my way.

Sometimes in the sweat lodge you are given an offering, some tobacco or a piece of cloth, and asked to pray for somebody. Afterwards, these offerings are placed in trees, so the spirits can hear the prayers.

I make offerings whenever I'm taking something from the land. This seems superstitious to some people, but for me it's a matter of being considerate and courteous. The law of Karma applies to our relationship with all of creation, not just humans. If we mistreat plants and animals and pollute the environment, why should we expect the earth to care for us, or tolerate our presence? When I kill deer or elk, I apologize to them, and thank them. I burn some sweetgrass and sage and smudge them with it. I put some cornmeal in their mouths. I cut a piece of their heart and put it in a bandana with a little tobacco. I tie it to a tree, to honor their spirits and the spirit of the place. I believe if I do this the animal's spirit won't be offended or afraid; it will come back so I can hunt it again.

When the huckleberries are ripe and we go out picking the first time, I go off by myself and pray to their spirit, the spirit of the soil, the rotting logs that make the soil, the rain that makes them grow, the clouds that bring the rain, the wind that carries the clouds. And if there's bears around I tell them we don't want to bother them and I ask them to leave us alone. When I pick serviceberries and chokecherries I make offerings and talk to the trees so they'll continue to bear fruit.

Before I start a logging project I go over to a place I won't disturb. I smudge and make an offering. I ask the spirits of that place to understand that my intentions are good, that I want to help the forest, not destroy it. I ask them to guide me, so I can make good decisions, and to watch over me to keep me safe. When I'm finished I go to back to that place and make another offering, and I thank them. Honoring the spirits, and working with them, helps me keep everything in perspective; I'm more concerned with leaving trees than cutting them, less concerned with making a profit than working with the least possible harm. This might not seem like a good business model, but I stay busy. Most people like the way the forest looks when I'm finished; they'll often say, "It looks so natural." That's because I let the spirits guide me. I try not to get in their way too much.

Inez and I grow sweetgrass and give it to people. We could sell it for a good price, but that would take the magic and power out of the whole process. The sweetgrass doesn't need much care other than watering and light weeding. But it likes to be tended and fussed over. I visit with it when it's growing, and when it's time to cut it, I smudge it, pray and make offerings. I explain what I'm about to do, apologize, and ask the sweetgrass to share its spirit with whomever uses it. I do the same thing when I gather cedar and sage for smudging, or sweet pine boughs to make a splasher for the sweat.

Dreaming is important to me. I've always had dreams where humans and animals become one another. When I'm hunting I'll dream about where I'll find a deer or an elk, and how I'll kill one. I see the future in dreams and experience past lives. When I was really young I dreamed of flying on a heron. When I have a hard decision to make, or if I'm unsure about what I'm doing,

I see herons. They give me a sense of security. I had to do a big remodel of our house once. It was going to be expensive and time-consuming and I really didn't want to tear the old part down because it had been our home for several years. I was at the kitchen table drawing plans one morning, stressing out over the cost. A heron flew past the window and sat in a lodgepole by the garden. He stayed there for about five minutes and left. I returned to the planning, knowing everything would work out. Walking out to my cabin later I found one of his feathers on the path. I keep it in the window above my desk.

I have an affinity for ravens. They're skittish around most people but they're not afraid of me. I feed them because I like to have them around. Like the herons, they appear at important moments, but more frequently. A few days after my friend Bud died I went to the place near my cabin. That morning I was thinking of Bud, honoring his spirit. When I was finished two ravens flew in and sat in a lodgepole, looking at me. They were showing me how Bud and I were still connected, even though he had died. When our friends Steve and Kerrie got married in the woods behind our house, two ravens circled overhead as we performed the ceremony. When Kerrie died we buried her not far from where she'd been married. I watched for some sign from the ravens all day while I made preparations, but never noticed anything. Just before dark, after almost everyone had left, I walked over to the grave, and found a raven tail feather lying in the trail. It didn't surprise me.

Sometimes ravens help me when I'm hunting. They get my attention and I follow them to where the elk are. Coyotes are also good guides. If I can't find game I'll follow a coyote track. He's a better hunter than me and knows where the food is. Like ravens, coyotes are extra sensitive and intelligent. They usually run from people, but if you don't mean them any harm they'll just sit and look at you, even if you have a rifle. Animals will guide you if you let them. Once, on a canoe trip in Saskatchewan, I was fishing for supper just before dark. It was too windy to get out on the lake, so I had to fish from shore. I waded out into the water so I could cast my spoon further. It wasn't a very promising spot, but I thought I could catch some small pike. There was a loon about forty yards out in the bay who started calling when he saw me. Normally they fly away, but this one stayed where he was. I worked the spoon along the shoreline first and then started casting into the deeper water. The loon didn't move, even though I was casting closer to him. I hooked a fish about twenty feet from him and took it back to shore. When I waded back out into the lake the loon had moved to my right. He was still calling but wasn't alarmed. I cast over near him and hooked another pike. I kept casting wherever he moved until I had four pike, which was all we needed for supper. My traveling companions were impressed with my fishing prowess, but I gave most of the credit to the loon; he told me where to fish.

I'm writing this about one month after I had brain surgery to fix a cerebral aneurysm. The operation was successful and I'm recuperating faster than I was expected to. Inez and I decided there were three reasons for this good outcome. First, I was healthy and strong. Second, the surgeon and his team were exceptional. And finally, but not least, people prayed for us. Each person had his own way, depending on their concept of prayer. Some were praying to God; others were sending good energy to us. Some of our friends who follow the Pipe Way prayed with their pipes and made offerings. One of them said "I'll send that Eagle with you. He's the most powerful.," and we saw eagles the whole way to Snoqualmie, when night fell. The eagles were a manifestation of the energy being sent our way, but we didn't need to see anything to know that our relatives and friends were pulling for us. We could feel the power of their prayers, and we still can, helping us along like a tailwind.

I've shared some very private things in this essay. Writing it has been cathartic, but unsettling. For one thing, there's too many "I's" in the text. For another, I worry that talking about these things might be a jinx. But mostly I wonder what the point is: who cares about my crackpot ideas and makeshift ceremonies?

I'm not a Protestant, Native American, or a Buddhist. I'm not a healer or a holy man or trained in any tradition. But I love my wife, my children, my family and my friends. I love the earth, the sky, the rivers, the seas, the forests, the mountains and the prairies, and I love all the creatures who live with us. I feel the spirit flowing through it all. I can't help it. These words are a cup I dip in that river of spirit. Here, have a drink.

November 2011

How Language Came to Humans

COYOTE LOOKED AROUND. As far as he could see, in every direction, the earth was steaming. Black pools of water boiled on the rocks. He walked over the world, tapping a stick as he went along. He walked through the steam, inhaling the earth's breath.

Coyote was lonely, because he was the only one. He looked at his shadow, reached down and cupped it in his paws, and breathed into it once, twice, three times, four times. Raven flew out, blinking his eyes in the sunlight. Coyote said "You are Raven. I have created you. You are black like the night that lives in the sun. You are magical because only you can do that." He told Raven, "Go, fly up and bring me a piece of the sun." Raven flew into the sun and returned with a tiny star glowing in his beak. It was so bright that Coyote had to put his paws over his eyes. He said, "Stand Back!" and hit the star with his stick. It shattered into millions of new stars. They flew into the sky and rained down on Coyote and Raven. Their light splashed over the newborn rocks, painting them with brilliant glowing colors.

Coyote told Raven, "Gather these stars and fly. Whenever you see a pool of water drop four of them in." Raven flew off and did what Coyote said. Coyote walked along below. When he saw fire in the water he stirred it with his stick, and two beings would be born in there. When they were fully formed he tapped at the water with his paw, and said "You are Bear," and two Bears appeared, with stars for eyes. Or he might say, "You are Bobcat," and two Bobcats emerged from the water, their eyes burning green. He walked around like this filling the world with all the beings we know. Humans were no different. Coyote said, "You are Humans" and We appeared. He walked away, and went on creating.

Coyote was the only one who could talk. Whatever he said happened. Whatever he thought happened. His words and thoughts had power because the Spirits of the Earth thought and acted through him. The other animals could speak without language, so they didn't need words. People could also do this, but they were curious. They were always asking questions, or answering them, and they craved Coyote's power. So they went to Raven, who was mischievous and canny, and asked him to steal Coyote's Medicine. They said, "If you help us we will speak the words that will change you into Eagle." Raven thought about it—he pictured himself with keener eyes, longer talons, broader wings, brilliant feathers, and a fierce, piercing call—and he agreed to steal Coyote's voice.

One afternoon Coyote had eaten his fill of strawberries, and he was napping in the sun. There wasn't anything for him to do since he'd filled the world with creatures. Raven circled above him, acting like he was just enjoying the day. When he saw that Coyote's mouth was wide open, his teeth stained red with berry juice, he was certain that Coyote was sleeping. He hurried back to the people and said, "Now's our chance!" So they snuck up on Coyote and pounced on him, pinning him down. Raven flew into Coyote's mouth, caught Coyote's voice, and flew out before Coyote could bite him. The people scattered and ran away. Coyote was too sleepy and sluggish to chase them very far, so after a little while he just sat down and yelled after them. But all that came out was a thin, yipping howl.

Coyote considered destroying the world right then, but he loved the innocent plants and animals. He loved the people too, but he wanted to teach them a lesson. Even though he couldn't speak, his thoughts could still make things happen. He thought: "They can talk until their tongues bleed. They can talk until they choke on their words. But their words will make it harder for them to visit with the Spirits who can help them live in a good way and trick them into believing they don't need this help."

When the people were all gathered back at their camp Raven gave them Coyote's voice. He said "Now, make me Eagle." A man said, "You are Eagle." Nothing happened. Then a woman tried. She said, "You are Eagle." Nothing happened. No matter who said it, or how many times they said it, Raven was still Raven, with the same old black feathers and the raspy croaking voice. Raven cocked his head and looked at them. He said, "I guess you're not as clever as you think you are," and flew off to look for Coyote.

Raven and Coyote went up to the highest mountain. There were no hard feelings between them. They just sat there and watched the world below. The plants and animals were content, but the people were wandering around, yakking all the time. Raven and Coyote didn't think Humans would be around much longer; they were so confused and distracted by their talking. But sometimes they heard drumming, and people singing from their hearts, singing songs without words, asking the Spirits to pray with them. And when they heard those songs Raven and Coyote thought humans just might survive, in spite of themselves.

1974

Acknowledgments

Poems and essays in this collection have appeared in the following publications:

Bugle magazine (Rocky Mountain Elk Foundation)

"Signatures on the Land"	Nov/Dec 1998
"Communion"	May/June 2000
"Thirty Quart Bucks"	July/Aug 2001
"Big Hole Afternoon"	Jan/Feb 2002

The Roadless Yaak *anthology*   2002

"The Loggers"

Montana Outdoors

"Grandpa's Gun"   Sep/Oct 2012

Whitefish Review

"Mousetrap"	2009
"Lodgepole"	2014

Many thanks to Bob & Susan Arnold at **Longhouse** in Green River, Vermont, who first published some of these poems in finely printed booklets.

"Saskatchewan Waters"
"Kinnikinnick"

About the Author

Bob and Inez Love live in northwest Montana near the confluence of the North and Middle forks of the Flathead River. They have two children, Orion and Keeley, and three grandsons, Henry, Augie and Ford. Bob is the owner and sole employee of Confluence Timber Company.

Bob Love standing on the far right with his first-grade class outside the Beaver County, Pennsylvania, Jail, circa 1959. Bob's teacher, Mrs. Dowd, thought a jail tour might be in order after some of the boys were collared by the town constable for disrupting legal proceedings—on several occasions—by running and yelling through the main hall of the courthouse on the way home from school.

Made in the USA
Monee, IL
09 March 2023